PHILIP...
JOHN 14 18...
JEREMIAH 17 9
EPHESIANS 2 10 JOSHUA 1 9
1 PETER 5 8
PROVERBS 11 2
MATTHEW 6 27

JOHN 6 37
JOHN...
MATTHEW 11 28
GALATIANS 51
PSALM 147 3
JEREMIAH 29 11
JOHN 16 33
ROMANS 12 2

1 PETER 2...
MATTHEW

OVERCOME

Father, I only exist because of You and Your grace. By all accounts, I should have been dead many years ago or at the very least, finishing my existence in prison. It is only by Your grace that my life has found purpose. However, I am completely unable to live this life on my own. I am awkward and get in the way far too often. Please use my flaws to strengthen a deeper reliance on You to do the work You have called me to. Please prepare my mind and my heart, by providing the tools, resources, and knowledge for how to best use them.

Thank You, Lord,

Amen.

OVERCOME

Biblical Responses to Destructive Reactions

Personal Edition

Joshua Staton

Overcome: Biblical Responses to Destructive Reactions – Personal Edition
Copyright © 2021 Joshua Staton
ISBN: 9781736963906

Cabin in the Woods Publishers, LLC
205 Deep Gap Loop Road
Flat Rock, North Carolina 28731
info@cabininthewoodspublishers.com
www.cabininthewoodspublishers.com
@cabininthewoodpublishers

A WORD OF THANKS

T hank yous are one of those courtesies that typically feel obligatory and mainly an exercise in exhibiting manners. With that being said, every once in a while, people come along who truly deserve to be recognized and thanked for their labor, assistance, and support. The following names not only represent a physical person but a precious soul whom God has weaved into my life for reasons I am still uncovering today. These are people who have been a blessing to me through their patient encouragement, faithful teaching, and so much more.

Looking back, my wife Kodi has proven to be my spiritual elder. She is steeped in scripture and is making every effort to live her life according to God's design. Without her faithful obedience to God, I am not sure I would even be here today. God used her faithfulness to reach me, and for that, words will always fail to express my gratitude.

If it were not for Chastity Bloomfield, I am fairly certain I would have never darkened the doorway of a support group meeting. She suggested that I come check out a substance abuse ministry that needed guys to help be mentors. I showed up one night and here we are, many years later. So, blame her. But in all seriousness, her godly influence reaches far and wide, in our community.

Many thanks are also due to Craig Halford at First Contact Ministries for accepting me into that ministry and providing opportunities to not only coach but to develop and lead a class. He has been a driving force for substance abuse ministries in our community and continues to expand his scope of impact and influence nationwide.

A few years ago, I met a man (who would eventually become my pastor) named Marcus D. Hayes. Every so often, you cross paths with someone who inspires you to follow Jesus all the more intensely and encourages you to live out the gospel more passionately. Pastor Marcus was that guy for me. He is now the lead pastor at Crossroads Baptist Church in Texas, and I am blessed to have his spiritual insight provide the foreword for this edition.

A word of thanks is also due to the many volunteers who have dedicated their time and invested their heart in the various addiction ministries not only in Western North Carolina but around the United States and the world. These *local* missionaries have sacrificed many creature comforts in exchange to be on the front lines, fighting this spiritual war. While it is a noble act to empathize with someone who is struggling with addiction, these soldiers were willing to revisit the smoke-laden trenches and fight to free those still enslaved. It is a convicting reality check to witness, and I cannot thank them all adequately enough.

And finally, I have the honor of thanking the many contributors who have volunteered their stories of redemption and spiritual healing as a testament to the transformative salvation of God:

Steve Booher, Tara Escobar, Lynette Oliver, Kevin Varble, Diane Hendrickson, Brooks Lancaster, Christine Parris, Ron Goss, Joseph M. Bohren, Chastity Bloomfield, Beth Blackwell, Chaz Jackson, Melia Huntley, Kodi Staton, David Marsh, and Adam McCraw.

Each one of these stories represents a life changed by the gospel. It is in these intimate glimpses of lives redeemed that we see the heart of God at work. I thank them for their willingness to share their suffering and salvation, with the hopes of reaching others who may be traveling similar paths. They are the hands and feet of Christ and I pray God continues to bless them for *embracing the awkward*.

CONTENTS

Foreword

Many times in life, people tend to shortcut a process. Me personally, I've seen it on the football field. Having played for many years in California and Oklahoma, I've watched my good friends not want to practice but want to play in the game. Or even something that was more dangerous – they would skip our weight room session and still try to play at a high level – very hard to do. It's like many other things in life, if you choose to skip key or important steps in a process it could be detrimental or essentially counter-productive.

In this book, my good friend Joshua Staton deals with just that. For a person on a quest to be set free from any addiction(s), the most important thing to consider is their spiritual condition first. Too often you see people desire to be "set free", but not deal with the greater need in their lives: their soul. I am a firm believer that if you want to see results in other areas of your life, you must first ask the question, "What's the condition of my soul?" For the record, I'm not talking about deep meditation, self-help methods, or religion. I am talking about having a personal relationship with Jesus Christ.

God sent His only son to the earth to fix what was wrong. Not that it was God's fault, but it was man's fault. In the garden of Eden, Adam and Eve chose to disobey God's one command and from that point, we have seen the results. Sin and the result of sin – death. However, since that point in history, mankind has tried to fill the void in their life with things from the world: success, relationships, drugs, work, material things, religion, and the list goes on. But we can't *fix* it. It is a God-size hole that Jesus filled when He died on the cross for our sins.

Paul the apostle writes in Galatians 5:1, "For freedom Christ has set you free, stand firm therefore, and do not submit again to a yoke of slavery." You see, if any person desires to be truly free and live the life God has intended them to live, it starts with the soul. In this book, Joshua will take us on a journey dealing with addiction, yet dealing with the deeper issue at hand, and that is ones' soul-care, their personal relationship with Jesus. Once you pick up this book and start reading it you will not want to put it down. My prayer for you as you read this book is that you will sense a deeper hunger than "merely" being set free from an addiction – which is important – but that you will surrender your life to Jesus Christ. God bless.

Pastor Marcus D. Hayes
Crossroads Baptist Church

Prologue

TIME TICKS BY

Many years have passed since I initially sat down at this kitchen table and engaged in what would become an ongoing war of words. The main battle was, and still is, the determination of what to say and how to say it. This moment of reminiscing provoked hellishly nostalgic memories of the various struggles I was entangled with over the past decade. When one of these particular clashes resulted in the calculated decision to end my life. Internal reckoning and constant disconnection signaled it was indeed past time to clock out. I was physically depleted and spiritually exhausted. Having failed to find any relevant significance for my existence, I put pen to paper to deliver the reasoning for my last goodbyes, which began with:

> "But here I sit writing, which is testament enough that something has gone horribly astray, somewhere along the way. My soul is dreadfully tired…"

I was not a follower of Christ for the first 32 disastrous years of my savage life. In all actuality, I was proud to call myself an atheist. In my early teens, I began self-medicating with alcohol to numb the pain of life, which began a devastating progression into various other drugs and a lifestyle that required pharmaceutical methamphetamines in the morning and pain killers throughout the day just to remain somewhat functional. This cycle repeated six to seven days a week for almost two decades.

Getting sober was not quick and easy. Establishing priorities wasn't a walk in the park neither. The first year was brutal, especially when you have alienated your closest friends and family. And this is where God found me; with nowhere to turn but to Him. Since I lacked earthly guidance and encouragement (repercussions of my own decisions), I formed the opinion that support groups only existed for weak-willed people. If you were serious about getting clean or sober you would commit to it, whether someone was cheering you on or not. As previously stated, these were my personal opinions; faulty and prideful.

About two years into recovery, a friend of my wife mentioned that a ministry she had been volunteering with needed guys to be coaches for their substance abuse program. Not knowing any better I said yes. After a few months, the man that founded that ministry asked if I would be interested in teaching a class. So, I sat at this same kitchen table over a Christmas break developing what I thought would be a support group that even I would want to go to.

ON THE SUBJECT OF SUFFERING
I am not what people would call a *compassionate* person. A classically trained teacher I am not, nor do I feel inherently equipped to be a leader or even a motivational speaker. I am not an expert, nor are there diplomas and certificates decorating the office walls, glorifying my accomplishments. Truth be told, this admitted deficiency probably makes me the least qualified person (now that I think about it, in this regard) to write about addiction and recovery. Sadly though, that does not make me any less responsible. Because woefully in my world, if you are aware of a piece of

information, you are then responsible for what you choose to do or not do with that knowledge.

I am however an observer and a writer. What can be offered are observations and analysis on life and confess where self-centered worldly logic and common sense have failed to produce acceptable answers. Not every situation or outcome in life is going to make sense. In fact, much of life doesn't compute; mostly because we live in a fallen world corrupted by sins that we all have contributed to. Tragedies happen to superheroes, and villains catch a lucky break every now and then. The hardworking folks of one generation get dismissed as relics, while others who backstab and dawdle seem to always hit the jackpot. Some children have everything handed to them just to squander it, while other kids come from broken homes into the foster care system and only want someone to play ball with or tuck them into bed at night. And at the same time, people who win the lottery turn around and gamble it all away at the casino, while families in dilapidated villages across the world die every day from common diseases and sickness that could have been treated had a generous benefactor been found. However, please do not confuse what is being communicated. I am not a socialist nor do I identify with any left or right, north or south, red or blue. These statements are not politically motivated. They are a nature of something a little more critical – our spiritual health as individuals and communities.

If you are an addict, you are naturally going to devote your life to something. We are not like other people. I believe when spiritually directed, the mental facilities of an addict have far greater potential than most any other type of mind. It is not by coincidence or accident that God has given you an inherent desire to dedicate yourself to pursuits. What we want to do is re-focus that urge. We are investments; invested with souls, talents, and passions to realize our potential and bring glory to our Creator. But for most of us, we go our entire life without realizing what we have been given, let alone what we should do with it. Without direction, we soon end up lost and try to navigate life with faulty information and guidance from a fallen world.

Tragically, we get distracted and discouraged by things that falsely seem significant and bring us temporary relief. We eventually look for anything to fill the desolation, for something to remedy our pain, all while ignoring the Truth that can truly heal. Soon, everything we use to fill our emptiness only makes the void that much deeper and harder to satisfy, like a spiritual sinkhole.

While I do not claim to explicitly know every human story, I am familiar with the commonalities, distractions, and the stage that it takes place on. If you expect things on Earth to make sense or fulfill you, you are going to be disappointed. The waiting room is packed with souls who have discovered this desolate revelation. A revelation that began with a sinking awareness that you may have sensed during childhood, felt in your teen years, and resentfully embraced in your adult years – the heartbreaking news that some (if not all) of your hopes and dreams may not come true.

These unfulfilled expectations then alchemize from hopeful fantasy to dreadful reality. Demonstrated through displayed instances like "no chance in hell reconciliation with specific family members, never getting the apology you feel you deserve, failing to be recognized for all your hard work, the never-ending fights with your spouse that show no signs of letting up, one more misstep and you'll be out on the street, you have no choice but to raise this kid all by yourself, things are not going to get any better no matter how hard you try, you will always carry a label and be judged because of it, all the investment and effort has been for nothing." These are lies aimed toward producing fatal desperation and many have sold everything precious in their life to buy this perishing stock.

These lies are found hiding in the fact that we are looking for earthly solutions to satisfy a spiritual problem that has originated from a deficit within the soul. Hopelessly, the longer we hold tight to the accepted promise that the distractions will fix our deficiencies, it inevitably gives way to needing more and more, permitting matters to increasingly worsen. Complications then arise when we are unable to fathom the thought of having to do without our distractions. The mind recoils in horror at the mere mention of having to find another way. We attempt to take ownership of our solution when in reality our solution now owns us. Curiously, we want to believe the lie that we can find joy and meaning in life from this world and what it offers, instead of a relationship with our Creator and Savior.

IN THE TRENCHES

We are a hurting people. We hurt each other and we hurt ourselves. This book wasn't written to make you feel good about bad choices or give you a get out of jail free card for the past. There is nothing I can say or write that will persuade you to believe that some decisions need to be re-evaluated and maybe you should consider willingly volunteering an upheaval of everything you feel about life. I can speculate and try to cover as many bases as possible, but the fact of the matter is our existence is so vast I will never be able to pinpoint exactly where and why life ran off the tracks. We are a messy and complicated species.

What I can do is give you an understanding of what this book is and what it is not. It is not *10 Ways to Find Happiness in Life*, or *Top 5 Life Hacks*, nor even *3 Fool-Proof Methods for Getting Your Sh*t Together*. It is not self-help literature or even a feel-good coming-of-age tale about a girl and a boy. It is about the spiritual trenches we find ourselves fighting in, day in and day out, the exhausting grind we resort to, and why we must come to digest the fact that we were not created to live life by seeking to fill this deep spiritual void within our hearts by whatever methods or means available. That sort of opportunistic approach will only lead to a confusing bird's nest of a headache when it comes time to sort it all out. This book will attempt to encourage you to switch weapons and tactics by teaching you how to fight in these trenches by replacing the all too familiar and destructive reactions with biblical responses.

In a broad sense, *Overcome*, is a strategic and topical platform designed to illuminate and confront any addictive sin that has destroyed your life or that you are on the path to destruction with. Mistakenly, many a functioning addict believes their sort of lifestyle is manageable. This logical error wrongly presumes that one is required to be spiraling out of control before countermeasures are warranted. Fundamentally, addiction is yet another expression of sin – another idol we allow and even encourage to take God's place in our hearts. That is what sin does, it wants to sit on the throne. This can be done with alcohol or gambling, lust or methamphetamines, heroin or envy. Anything that creates a disturbance in your life and sends you down the wrong paths that can potentially lead to cataclysmic disaster. Make no mistake, you are in a war. You will be guaranteed to fight battles at times on this journey. But rejoice in the fact that you are not obligated to fight alone.

The intent of this book (as with all discipleship) is to provide applicable education regarding natural humanistic reactions and encourage us to respond by actively engaging in our recovery and walk with Christ. Because at the end of the day, we are commanded to love others and make disciples. The way we do this is by loving people where they are but loving them enough to not just leave them there. Jesus called His twelve disciples from where they were. There was no *Galilee's Got Talent* to find the most articulate, attractive, or even the most equipped contestants. Why? Because the gospel is not about us and what we can do, it is about Him and what He has done and continues to do, even to this very day. He is in the business of redeeming and re-purposing lost souls. Granted, we may have been sinners and addicts, but He has called us to a greater significance; to become His saints.

Ultimately, recovery is not solely about removing drugs and alcohol from your life. It is about the transformation from death and destruction to eternal life through the gospel. Subtraction by itself does not a balanced equation make, addition must also occur.

"When the unclean spirit has gone out of a person, it passes through waterless places seeking rest, but finds none. Then it says, 'I will return to my house from which I came.' And when it comes, it finds the house empty, swept, and put in order. Then it goes and brings with it seven other spirits more evil than itself, and they enter and dwell there, and the last state of that person is worse than the first."

Matthew 12:43-45a

FRAMEWORK

The premise for Overcome is rather straightforward; addiction is a side effect of a much larger issue. Usually, a lot of hidden issues that act as motivations for addictive behavior, which are addressed in 17 topical chapters. There was no way to be all-inclusive when discussing the motivations. If we were, this book would go on forever.

Nevertheless, observations led me to see certain trends in emotional reactions that resulted from circumstances – and in many cases, continuous strings of events. These situations could have turned out much differently if only a few mature thoughts and what the Bible calls wisdom and discretion were practiced. I, however, have realized I am always going to have the need to pour myself into something – good or bad. Option A says I can choose to fight this personality flaw and live a crippling existence mired down by restraint. Option B allows me to embrace this need by seeking God to provide a better blueprint for its usage. Tip: pick B.

In all honesty, the creation of the original curriculum and the requirements that it needed to meet was not as simple as I would have preferred. In substance abuse ministries, individuals coming in could spiritually range anywhere from the 'unchurched', to Catholic, to atheist. Some were fresh out of rehab and eager, while others were still high when they walked in off the street. Some were tourists that may not make it to every meeting while others would show up halfway through the semester. As much as I would have liked to sit down and fashioned this as a successively developing class, I was not able to. Each session had to stand on its own and be flexible enough that newcomers would not be lost walking in halfway through the semester.

The way this challenging opportunity was approached was to identify human and spiritual commonalities. This was done by unpacking a destructive motivating factor (or by-product) of addiction – such as isolation – and juxtapose a biblical response to it. We then looked for scripture to provide a biblical lens on how to view and address the particular topic (in the case of isolation, it was to encourage ways to focus on others). Additionally, we found tragic stories of famous individuals whose lives were lost to addiction and made observations to certain trends or mind space, which was then contrasted with a testimony from another individual who had found freedom from their addiction. Since 2013, Overcome has continued to evolve from an experimental support group into what you are now reading. It has been adopted by ministries and non-profits nationwide as a platform to engage in supportive discipleship for these precious souls struggling with addiction and recovery.

ABOUT THIS EDITION

The decision to provide a personal edition of Overcome was not on my immediate radar nor my to-do list. In fact, I was fairly apprehensive when asked, "Have you thought about doing a student edition?" My hesitancy resided in the belief (or in this case, supposed knowledge) that the reason why it worked was because of the people sitting around the tables and the dynamics of the group. I honestly cringed at the thought of having to figure out how to capture that essence in a purely written form and then convey it to the reader, who may be sitting alone at home, riding a bus somewhere, on their lunch break or sitting in a 10x10.

Still, time passed and continued to bring requests for a personal edition. So, I reluctantly grabbed a copy of the leader's edition and started thumbing through it trying to figure out how to make this transition as painless as possible. While flipping through the pages, two things occurred. The first was the realization that the truth of God's Word is not subject to location, circumstance, or personality. It is just as relevant now as it was then. It is all the more crucial *here* as it was *there*. It contains the same power despite who is reading it or where they are reading it.

The second realization was the fact that a portion of these personal dynamics could be brought into book form. So, a request was put out to friends and various communities of substance abuse ministries, and it was remarkably answered. At the end of each chapter, you will find an inspirational snapshot provided by an individual who has agreed to share their experiences with substance abuse and the redemption God offers through Jesus. I pray that you find a story you can relate to, but above and beyond that, I hope you find encouragement for continuing your journey through recovery. We all have a purpose here on this planet. While we may not have been the best stewards of this opportunity and responsibility in the past, God gives grace. But it is up to us to embrace it and make the most of it.

A GOD OF REDEMPTION

Many years have evaporated into the ether since we began this journey of recovery support, stumbling at times along the way. Sometimes, we stood back up with a passion, and other times we barely beat the ten-count. Occasionally, we have risen a little worse for the wear, but we eventually rose stronger. The important part is that we got back up again. It is in these moments that we find both the limits of human effort as well as the depth of God's divinity; a reality and a choice we experience every time we fall. I admit, it is easier to lay there after being knocked down, but it is more painful and sickening to just watch it all fall apart.

Choosing to passively allow bedlam to consume your efforts is difficult to articulate but think of it like a *Choose Your Own Adventure* book, whereas you get to decide what path the story is going to take. Behind my grandmother's house, two creeks converged in a rather geologically odd confluence. The path of the first creek ran fairly straight, while the second creek formed a strange S-curve before joining up with the other one. At the intersection of this peculiar hydraulic marriage, a pseudo beach was formed, and the only way to get there was by jumping across the first creek. On the beach, you then had access to catching what we southerners call crawdads – for the uninitiated, think of them as mini-mountain lobsters. It was during one of these roundups that the idea materialized in my mind to build a dam. Specifically, a dam to bridge from the first bank across to the island. Little did I know at that age, it was not wise to block the only means of escape for the flow of two creeks.

Almost fifty yards downstream from the dam was a culvert, just slightly bigger in diameter than a 55-gallon drum. After spending an almost entirely rainless summer constructing that dam, the unthinkable happened. It rained. And rained. And rained. The dam, being built from every rock I could find (including those from the creek beds, the beach, and ones dug out of the bank sides) held back the torrential downpour for the first few days. But as the rain continued to fall, and the water in both creeks rapidly rose, I started noticing the accumulated water was now carving out the banks under small trees and bushes along the sides of the creek.

In hindsight, this should have been a warning sign that what I had built would soon lead to a disastrous chain reaction. The domino effect began with the dam collecting the eroded small bushes and clumps of battered leaves (impressively preventing what little water was previously permitted to escape) which provided just enough blockage for the onslaught of rushing water to carefully extract a few rocks, at first. Then, the water violently decimated the pile of stones, which were now in the process of being relocated to the mouth of the culvert. I know all of this because I sat there watching it happen and did nothing to avert the eventual destruction of the road that the culvert ran under.

We all have obviously started out as something much different than what we have become. Even though we may find ourselves presently in bad situations, it does not mean that is the end of the story. This awareness, over time, has forced me to acknowledge that I do not indeed know it all, nor can I provide a suitable answer for the suffering you may be experiencing right now. But I can offer the following perspective:

I have seen sunny days deliver dark news. I have witnessed rain bring about deep spiritual growth. I have seen a dog covered in cancer (one heartbreaking decision away from being put down) who would eventually recover and regain spirit in his step. I have seen employees with tattoos all over their faces model the loving leadership of Jesus towards supervisors wearing collared shirts. I have seen our Lord bring addicts back from dark valleys who are now preaching and teaching the word of God.

And I have seen this kitchen table when it looked brand new. However, it is disproportionately worn and haggard now. There is nothing particularly fancy about it, and if memory serves accurately, we bought it at a thrift store almost a decade ago for $10 and refinished it. It is rickety and creaks when you put weight on it, and the varnish has since faded. There are chunks of mac and cheese (I hope that is what it is) that need to be chiseled off because the kids have poor hand-eye-mouth coordination. It has seen many a hand of Rummy played on it, a Thanksgiving or two, a few Christmas mornings, countless discussions, and a goodbye letter written on it. It has seen its fair share of use since that original battle, but it still serves its intended purpose.

We too all have a purpose, a heavenly one. Be that as it may, it will be your decision if you choose to leave those spiritual wastelands you may be inhabiting and search for that heavenly purpose. If you consign to take that first step, then I wish you safety and endurance on your journey, my fellow pilgrims.

JOHN 6 37

PHILIPPIANS 1 6

JOHN 14 18

JEREMIAH 17 9

1 PETER 2 11

MATTHEW 6 33

JOSHUA 1 9

OV
ER
CO
ME

JEREMIAH 29 11

GALATIANS 5 1

PROVERBS 11 2

MATTHEW 11 28

EPHESIANS 2 10

1 PETER 5 8

PSALM 147 3

MATTHEW 6 27

JOHN 16 33

ROMANS 12 2

I

Isolation and Encouragement

ROTTING FRUIT ON THE VINE

There is nothing more disheartening or defeating than for a farmer to look out on his orchards and see fruit rotting on the vines. This is a two-fold failure; wasted exertion on his part and wasted resources that could have gone to a venture possibly more productive. It is not that the tree is incapable of producing fruit, it has simply been left abandoned. Fruit-bearing trees, much like us humans were not designed to operate in isolation. In fact, nothing in our universe is created to sustain itself or exist in lonesome confinement.

When someone does you wrong, and you experience injury, what is your primordial reaction? For many of us, it may be anger or sadness, but for some our initial reaction is to withdraw. We detach from everything, including God. When we isolate, we concentrate on the offense and foster an intense focus on the self. We become near-sighted, so much so, that we no longer look outside of ourselves. Eventually, the burden slowly becomes unbearable, and our foundation starts to crack under the compressive weight.

While the contrasts between introversion and extroversion are entertaining to discuss, they will unfortunately not factor into this examination of isolation. We will be talking about isolation as an emotional reaction to what another person may or may not have done. It becomes an effect of an emotional reaction we have when we are hurt or rejected. I was angry with God for the biggest portion of my life and all I manufactured was destruction through rotten fruit.

An individual needs a correct godly perspective if they are to combat this deadly device used by our enemy. Satan's main objective is to separate us from others – to get us away from those who can speak grace, truth, compassion, guidance, and correction into our life – the ones that encourage us to keep walking. Their presence is then conveniently replaced by those who only seek to bring us down further. Misery loves company in that odd sadistic kind of way. We all need someone in our lives who is going to say, "Look, you're about to screw up", instead of instigating us to go further down the rabbit hole.

Part of undergoing this spiritual tilling in the field of our heart is to become increasingly aligned to the image of what God has designed us to be, based on what we produce. Although it may be a strain, we must endeavor to stop producing tainted fruit (as a result of our reactions to trouble) and begin bearing good fruit. Believe it or not, all struggles will elicit some form of outcome. This consequential response to difficulty is the same sort of trial that creates brilliant diamonds, moves pistons in combustion engines, and causes apples to spring forth.

JESUS REACHED OUT

I will not leave you as orphans; I will come to you.

John 14:18

We begin our study with the second shortest verse we will cover (and additionally, the shortest chapter of the book – it made sense to start gradually and build from there). And by all accounts, this is a relatively plainspoken and an easy one to memorize. The context of this scripture is what is ultimately pivotal. Jesus is delivering a promise to his followers during the last supper (typically referred to as the *upper room discourse*) and it is the promising of the Holy Spirit.

When I first became a Christ-follower, I was repeatedly told to hold on to God's promises. Pitifully though, I had no clue what they were talking about. No one specifically told me what they were, what they meant, or even where to find them. I know from personal experience when the darkness begins to slowly creep in, you need something to hold on to. You need shelter. You need an anchor. You need a *promise*. For all of us, God's promises must speak louder than the world if we are going to overcome anything.

> Knowing and believing what is in the Bible is the difference between being overcome by circumstances versus overcoming them.

Unfortunately, isolation is my preferred means of existence. For me, it is safer and comes with less headache (completely lazy and selfish, I will admit). It is quite clear and comfortable to diagnose if you are the one on the outside looking in, but almost impossible to recognize when you are the one who is down in the hole, disengaged from society, family, and friends. Why? Because isolation is a *justified* reaction. It is so ingrained in our thought process that it is the only logical conclusion, and it becomes a go-to defense mechanism when we need it. The harsh reality is learning to distinguish what occurs when we handle difficulties via means of isolation – the descent into darkness eventually becomes augmented and accelerated. When we isolate, we only seek to protect ourselves, which becomes a cyclical pattern that quickly mutates into a downward spiral. To break this sequence, we need to be purposeful and pursue relationships with others. Specifically, opportunities to connect, share and serve.

MISSING THE FOREST

At times, it is understandable how we can miss the forest because we are so concentrated on the trees. As a result of our preoccupation with disengaged abandonment, we lose sight of a very apparent and significant fact – every person has needs. The need to feel accepted, appreciated, important, and safe. And most of the time we look to the people around us to fulfill and validate those requirements. But we don't acknowledge they are more than likely dealing with the same needs. Instead, a fear exposes itself through our apprehension of meeting the needs of another person, that of neglecting our own. So, if this is the case, then what are we left to do? Something so completely counterintuitive that it may just be crazy enough to work: meet the needs of someone else.

How do we exit isolation and move to serve others? Sounds like a pretty cumbersome and misaligned task, doesn't it? Primarily, we should realize what happens when we isolate; we focus so intensely on ourselves and our conditions that we don't entertain thoughts of anything else. We are not just physically or mentally isolated, we are emotionally and spiritually separated. We become consumed by it, and in fact, many of the motivating factors we will cover throughout this book discuss this sort of unhealthy inward focus on ourselves.

Serving others can take many different forms – actions, words, and occasionally silent supportive presence. Examples range from simply holding a door for someone else, a courteous "Good morning", all the way to encouraging someone to keep doing well if you know they are struggling. Mostly everyone who has gone through recovery knows there is always that lurking feeling of loneliness. Part of recovery is not only being willing to have someone reach into your life but also being obedient to pour into someone else's as God directs. It will be the same feeling of loneliness that we felt at one time that will motivate us to be compassionate toward another person during their time of need. But we have to be willing to step outside ourselves long enough to notice the need.

Therefore encourage one another and build one another up, just as you are doing.

1 Thessalonians 5:11

Opening up your life and allowing someone else to know the grungy details takes a huge leap of faith and does not normally happen all at once. If you have withdrawn from your mission field – family, friends, coworkers – please understand that God has equipped you with a special story composed of all your hurts, struggles, and victories. He has given you talents, gifts, and a perspective to fulfill this great calling. And He has placed you in these locations and situations for a very specific purpose: His glory. All great journeys begin with a first trepid step, here is ours:

Seek one opportunity to serve someone else today.

Kodi Staton

> "I was born and raised in the church and have several pastors and preachers in my bloodline."

I was saved from hell around five years old. I knew fear and sadness and I saw pain and evil from my father towards my mother routinely – sunglasses to hide bruises on Sunday mornings.

I found refuge in the church, but by age 13, I was ready for an escape and found a good one in alcohol. I began binge drinking immediately. Puking made room for more and blackouts eventually led to sleep. I've asked forgiveness for whatever happened during those dark times (I still don't know to this day and maybe never will). Fights, depression, suicide attempts, wrecks, broken bones, near death, chaotic relationships, aimless jobs, and failed schooling; my solution never changed.

I still hoped there was more to life and signed up for a mission trip: babies unwanted, children dying, homeless, and hurting. My heart ached for others more than it did for myself. So, I changed careers, sought to help others; off and on drinking and still in dysfunctional relationships. My sober escape was out of the country serving others.

After another trip to the club and worn out from the empty search for happiness, my friend and I found a church in the yellow pages. The message the next day was about a master having two pots and one becomes broken and can't carry water. The broken pot cries out for the master to get a new one. The master shows the pot the flowers growing from the seeds the fractured pot has been watering along its way. I am that "cracked pot".

That began a change in my heart and mind and awakened something in my soul. Sunday after Sunday I couldn't stop the tears from flowing and the pastor's assistant, Tiffany, noticed me and began walking me through addiction material called "Inner Healing". I clung to God's truth and exchanged every hurt, fear, disappointment, unloved moment, sin, and evil in my life. For forgiveness, hope, and freedom. God had a purpose for my life and was preparing me to let Him use my darkness for good. He truly loved me and for the first time in my life, I believed it with my whole self. I poured myself into helping others and this was my new high. Helping the youth group, community service projects, every mission trip I could afford, bible studies, devotions, supporting others became my life.

In marriage, I brought my heart for helping others and my old friend alcohol. I quickly learned my husband shared my escapism but there was more violence and cruelty before the blackout. Something had to change, and my final sips were for any hope of saving our marriage and protecting myself. I ran to the lessons I clung to, the life-giving scriptures that changed my path. The secrets and lies were exposed and my heartbroken, broken for what I thought I had. Broken for what I wanted my marriage to be. I was ready for whatever was necessary. My husband entertained the small hope that God was for him and with him – and He was. With a hard road of healing ahead, our marriage continued, and we began helping others together.

Our house is fuller now and the mission trips are on hold, our family sponsors and helps the children I long to meet in distant countries and our greatest purpose lives under our very roof, our children are all from families looking for their own escape and freedom in alcohol and drugs, just like I did. It's hard and tiring and hopeful and freeing. If nothing else comes from my life, I am watering these seeds. I'm sharing God's truth – He loves us, He has a plan and purpose for our lives, and He is always with us.

OVERCOME

JOHN 6 37

PHILIPPIANS 1 6

JOHN 14 18

1 PETER 2 11

MATTHEW 6 33

JEREMIAH 17 9

JOSHUA 19

JEREMIAH 29 11

GALATIANS 5 1

PROVERBS 11 2

MATTHEW 11 28

EPHESIANS 2 10

1 PETER 5 8

PSALM 147 3

MATTHEW 6 27

JOHN 16 33

ROMANS 12 2

II

Rejection and Acceptance

IDENTITY CRISIS

W hat do we look to that is capable of providing our self-worth? For some, it may be their family and for others, it may be their car or career. Relationships, professions, and possessions will sooner or later fail in satisfying our need for validated acceptance. With an inaccurate view of our importance and worth, we regularly find ourselves engaging in activities we really don't want to, in hopes of obtaining love and a sense of belonging.

Rejection is a rather sensitive subject and should be handled accordingly, just like plutonium. To put it quite bluntly, as a doctor I have horrible bedside manner. Clinically, sometimes I tell people they just need to get over stuff. But in the case of rejection, this isn't an obstacle that you can just get over or go around. The only way past it is *through* it. Problems like these are not just going to go away. Unless we acknowledge the block and deal with it head-on, the result of this reactive attitude will always sabotage our intentions. Ignoring and trying to bury these feelings will only disguise them further.

THE SECURITY OF OUR IDENTITY

Topically, rejection and acceptance are substantial questions revolving around the security of our identity. The answer is found hidden in what we value, what we are willing to sacrifice for, and what we find our personal worth in. The easiest way to find out what we value is to complete the following statement by filling in the blank:

I am important because _____.

The specific dilemma of rejection was – and in many ways still is – one of the familiar demons that tormented me and conditioned the reaction to isolate permanently. It was only after becoming aware of rejection, did I see how much it poisoned life. Many of my actions were driven by the need to be accepted by the worlds' standards and by other humans, which was learned early on in childhood at home. That is why it is so consequential to acknowledge and address it as soon as possible before we reproduce it as adults. Because rejection not only as a child but as an adult will lead us to some pretty strange watering holes in the attempt to feel noticed and accepted.

We all have a worldly identity and a godly identity; and we are constantly building one or the other, with no exception. There will always be a gap between these two identities and depending on the circumstances, most of us will innately lean towards one or the other. The further we gravitate to one, the more acceptance we experience from it and subsequent rejection we feel from the other. Rejection is entrenching and generational. Rejection will undermine progress, motivation, and enthusiasm in your life. And most terminally, rejection breeds rejection just like a virus.

NAME TAGS

Some people are great at conversations, even with a complete stranger. They have this phenomenal ability to somehow transform a stranger into an old friend in under two minutes. If they are the superhero, then I am perceptibly closer to resembling the doleful sidekick who has already gone to the car and is waiting for them to hurry up so we can go get tacos. However, (whether we care to admit it or not) we are judging and assigning value to others all the time. The problem is that we usually do this subconsciously when assigning worth to what they value by asking internal qualifiers like, "How are we alike? Do I want to know more about them? Are they interesting? Does their crazy match my crazy?" In gauging them, we are subconsciously labeling (possibly wrongly) based solely on an impression.

Referring to this act of categorization, what labels has the world placed upon you? Were you known as the pothead, drunk, tweaker, a hoodlum, worthless? Write them down because we are going to come back to them in a moment and sort them all out but remember these are labels that the world has bestowed upon you with the sole intention of cramming you into a divisive mold.

When we attach labels, consciously or even subconsciously, we are judging and assigning value. In doing so, we initiate the process of justifying the rejection of others based on perception. However, when we do this to ourselves, we start to reject the future possibility of us because of the grimy and gritty past.

JESUS'S PROMISE

All that the Father gives me will come to me, and whoever comes to me I will never cast out.

John 6:37

To fully appreciate the context of this scripture, you are encouraged to read the entirety of chapter 6, but here is the build-up: Jesus has just fed five thousand people and performed many miracles. He is taking care of the earthly needs of His audience, but more importantly, He is promising to take care of their spiritual and eternal needs. The crowd appears to be receptive and loving Him. All that seems to be left to do is hold a formal ceremony, make Him their king, and free them from their Roman oppressors...

For our case, we need to notice the very first word in this verse – ALL. Many people adopt the false reality that they are required to somehow clean themselves up or become someone else before coming to Christ. The great news for us is that is not at all how it works – Jesus already knows all the grime and grit. After all, that's the reason He chose to die for us. Cleaning ourselves up isn't part of our job description, because we aren't qualified to do it. No offense, but that sort of thinking is like hiring a plumber to perform open-heart surgery. Sure, they both deal with plumbing, in a sense, but seems a little sketchy to me.

REJECTION OF JESUS
Picking back up in our verse of scripture, Jesus has fed a couple of thousand people and departed to the other side of the sea. The very next day, the crowds see Him on the other side and rush across the water to Him. However, He draws a line in the sand by saying that no one can come to the Father but through Him – whom the Father has sent. And before too long, the entire scene changes from upbeat and carefree to something much different – He eventually calls them out for only wanting what they can get from Him. By the end of John chapter 6, many of the ones looking to get something from Jesus would turn their back on Him and choose to no longer be a follower.

Be mindful, this rejection is coming from a group – a public crowd who didn't know or value Him. They came to Him for miracles (to be healed and fed), that was all they wanted. It was this sort of self-serving relationship that turned the crowds into consumers and Jesus into a service provider, rather than Lord and Savior. They followed Him not based on belief but instead because He met a temporary need. Instances like this illustrate what they thought Jesus was worth, and how deeply He knew rejection. It was even prophesied in the Old Testament book of Isaiah:

He was despised and rejected by men, a man of sorrows and acquainted with grief; and as one from whom men hide their faces he was despised, and we esteemed him not.

Isaiah 53:3

THE ADOPTION PROCESS

Earlier you were asked to write out the labels the world has given you. Despite whether those labels were rightfully earned or even warranted, they are reflective of the choices that Jesus died for to pay our debt and bring us back into a right relationship with the Father. The world will give us many labels throughout our lives, some fairly and some unfairly. Until we concede that each of us was paid for by the work of Jesus on the cross, we will never be able to adopt the new label of identity that He has gracefully given us.

Regretfully, it took two years in recovery to grasp just how much the feeling of rejection and the resulting resentment had indeed directed my atheism and hatred toward not only people but more wretchedly toward God. The rejection endured from my parents and family (which was wrongly interpreted as originating from God), created very thick callouses on my heart and the building up of walls, which were both painful in the forming and removal of.

As time progressed and the walls started coming down, I felt closer to God, but oddly, felt more further away from people than ever before. I was attempting to be a part of society again but just didn't feel accepted any longer. In hindsight, I now register the reasoning for this, but during the time it was going on, reminders of why the walls were even built in the first place became ever-present again. Then as arduous as that exercise was, it appeared the uphill climb was only getting underway.

There were many instances during that first year that I just wanted to give up on the idea of being a member of society or a family again. Constant criticism and judgmental attitudes were eroding my enthusiasm for this new and awkward endeavor. Then again, much like stopping a train, it doesn't just happen immediately. Turning that train around is even harder and takes a considerable amount of time and patience.

Repentance is not easy, in the same way, that flying is no effortless feat for humans. It is simple for a bird, but without an airplane or a blimp, we ain't making it to the clouds. Repentance is inhumanely torturous for one main reason; it requires that we admit our wrongs and surrender our agenda. This process is necessary though and is one of the methods God uses to manifest His ongoing work of aligning us incrementally more into the likeness of His Son.

After enduring the period of initial refinement, a most obvious glitch presented itself in such a subtle way, that it paralyzed my hand after writing it. Repeating itself in various forms throughout my journals, the question "What am I supposed to do with my life now?" stared back at me, waiting for a reply. For whatever reason, the give-me-something-to-do mentality is where we think we are doing right but proves itself to be a more capable hamster wheel than an outward reflection of gratefulness. Repeatedly, this line of reasoning is where I find myself veering off the tracks. Always drifting toward having to prove worthiness is a natural predilection of mine. I am not proud of it, nor ashamed of it. It is a foundational aspect of my personality. It is my 'thorn' in Paul's words. So much of my identity is tied up in activities and abilities that if 200% were not given, I would feel like a failure no matter the outcome.

Yet, our importance from Jesus is not based on our work but originates in our belief. His acceptance is not rooted in performance or achievement, but faith. It is not like waiting on a raise at work that never comes, approval from a spouse, or acceptance into some clique. It is the belief that Jesus is who He said He is, the way, the truth, and the life. And until we accept that, we may very well continue finding ourselves traveling down curvy and treacherous roads, that only lead to dead ends.

Pause for a moment and reflect over what we have discussed in this chapter so far regarding labels and identity. Earlier, you were asked to fill in a blank that would help define your identity by attributing a source of your worth. For many, it may be a role at work or responsibilities for your family. You were also asked to write down some of those labels that you have been given in the past. Bookmark those thoughts and look at our verse of scripture again for this chapter. There is one additional word we need to not only notice but appreciate.

All that the Father gives me will come to me, and whoever comes to me I will never cast out.

John 6:37

That word is WHOEVER. Take a pen and mark through each one of those labels the world has given you and write beside it, above it, or through it the word WHOEVER. The identity of our heavenly Savior is incomparable in value to whatever classification the world has saddled us with. Whether we worked long and hard to earn it and wear it like a badge of honor, or we are ashamed of it, and it is a reminder of the disgrace.

John 6:37 is a beautiful promise and proclamation that you are a unique and integral part of God's plan here on Earth. Trust in the promise that He will never cast you out. This promise is available to anyone. Race, gender, age, income, drunk or sober – none of these labels matter as much as the identity He gives us once we embrace His acceptance. To live out this identity first requires our belief that sin created a debt we can't pay. Once this is acknowledged, we trust that Jesus chose to pay our debt with His death because of His great love. We then choose to turn away from the source of that debt and follow Him. You are the whoever He spoke of.

Trust in the words ALL and WHOEVER.

Steve Booher

> "My addiction started out as trying to fit into a group of guys I played music with, in a rag-tag band of misfits."

Well, let me back up a little bit. My doctor would shoot me up with amphetamines for asthma – to clear my lungs. I suffered till I reached my teenage years.

Like most, I enjoyed the high and the false power that came with the speed. Life was a blur and then I got married (which only compounded the problem that I already wouldn't face). I stole my sister's meds and traded them for my dope. I worked three jobs to supply the needs of my family and my addiction. I tried religion, but it was not helping me at that time of my journey. I used God as a spare tire every time I got in a bind. One day it all crashed down as I went to the emergency room for what I thought was a pulled muscle.

Turns out I was having a heart attack from the street drugs I had been doing all day. After 5 bypass surgeries and 2 weeks in the hospital. I was faced with a life that had to change. I went through a rehabilitation program and got back to work. But had to resort to making $7.12 an hour, instead of the several hundred a week I was used to.

After five long years, I started drinking again. It was then I knew there must be a change. I was invited to church while at a birthday party and said I might go. That Sunday God woke me early and I went to church where I surrendered my life to the Lord Jesus Christ.

Now I was making different decisions and doing it sober. I started helping an outreach team and having early service with addicts in a detox facility. God put a love in my new heart for others hurting, just like I used to hurt. I then started helping at First Contact (a drug addiction ministry) and met several people who just needed a way out of their own turmoil and traps that held them in bondage.

I started helping Josh Staton with a class called Overcome. It met people right where they were and helped deal with a lot of life issues. I stayed in that class for 5 years and have seen a lot of guys use the lessons to tackle addiction, day by day. I believe that with the Overcome materials and the scriptures mixed in has been the key to the Lord helping a lot of people move forward in life and their healings.

I believe God sends people that are broken and hurting into a place of help so when they rise up, they can pull another person up with them. I am reminded daily that if you want grace and mercy, you must show it to others first. Love God and love people. The rest are minor details but put God first. He will work out all the other stuff. If you ask me, "How did I get clean and sober?" I would say it was by the blood of the Lamb and the words of my testimony. To God goes the glory. If you are considering a way out, God will produce a solid way for anyone who is ready.

For God so loved the world, that he gave his only Son, that whoever believes in him should not perish but have eternal life.

John 3:16

JOHN 6 37

PHILIPPIANS 16

JOHN 14 18

JEREMIAH 17 9

1 PETER 2 11

MATTHEW 6 33

JOSHUA 19

OVER
CO
ME

JEREMIAH 29 11

GALATIANS 51

PROVERBS 11 2

MATTHEW 11 28

EPHESIANS 2 10

1 PETER 58

PSALM 147 3

MATTHEW 6 27/8

JOHN 16 33

ROMANS 12 2

III

Depression and Hope

MADE OF HABITS

It is perfectly acceptable to be sad and sorrowful at times. But the danger discloses itself when you choose to stay there, eventually starting to feel as if you are trapped. Your perspective can become skewed, days teeter towards the dreary, and you begin to see life through gray-colored lenses. Depression, at times, resembles a gradual choice and a susceptibility rather than an unbreakable curse cast upon us. To buy into the lie that we aren't able to fight this antagonist is to give up on the hope for a better day.

I will let you in on a little secret before we get too far, I dislike (more like loathe) writing about depression for a very selfish and obvious reason. Depression is magnetic and the chance is always great that you will dig up old memories and get pulled into the gravitational vortex all over again after escaping the black hole the first time. It is surprisingly easy to entertain memories and subsequently find yourself dwelling on them and inadvertently re-living those sources of depression. While we will spend some time developing the segment for depression, we will be moving steadily towards applying the act of hope. Hang tight, there is a reason for this scenic route we are taking.

It is not accidental that the average age for onset of major persistent depression is around 29 to 32.5 years old. For many in our day and time, it is around this age when the idealized dream begins to deteriorate and the reality of adulthood sets in. Depression is clinically characterized by overwhelming sadness, low energy, loss of interest, anger, and anxiety. Not making light of the impediment, but I don't know many adults, specifically parents who don't chronically suffer from at least a few of these symptoms at any given moment. This is why the grounds for depression taking root are so fertile. Once the melancholy springs up and begins to blossom, it appears to be a result of the environmental needs and demands – physical, mental, spiritual, and emotional – we attempt to balance on a somewhat frequent basis. We find ourselves halfway to depression just by reaching a certain mile marker in life; even before we factor in events like past losses, responsibilities, and thought patterns that more than happily push us over the threshold.

DIAGNOSTICS

For our discussion, we will define depression as a habit of overwhelming thought that we find ourselves locked into, that establishes a perceived reality. The most effective way we can pinpoint the origin of depression is to treat it as if it were a rhetorical debate that we may not even be conscious or cognizant that we are asking and answering every time it barges in. An internal feeling that asks:

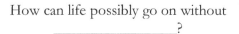

How can life possibly go on without
_____?

Take a moment and write down the areas of your life that generate feelings of hopelessness, despair, or discouragement. It is fairly obvious we don't get depressed about things we hold no particular interest in. We are disheartened over the losses of what we value: loss of a job, broken relationships, vacations ending, achievements (odd I know), unmet expectations, rejection, loneliness, poor decisions that caused pain to you or others, relinquishment of freedom or physical mobility, sickness, death of a loved one, and the feeling of social isolation.

Admittedly, we all have this perfect picture inside our minds of what we feel our life is supposed to look like. Oftentimes, plans don't go accordingly, and that picture never develops. When it doesn't, we find ourselves dwelling on these losses like a broken record reminding us of what could have been every time the needle skips. For some, it may be specific situations that are a little too familiar or certain seasons of the year that invite echoes of the past to revisit. This reverberation becomes a regular practice (willful or not) that diverges our focus, and we noticeably start to succumb. Addiction distracted me from processing the depressive memories. I believed in the picture I was painting; convinced it would make everything better, whether I admitted it or not.

Whoever gives thought to the word will discover good, and blessed is he who trusts in the Lord.

Proverbs 16:20

COMING TO TERMS

What is your basic reaction when you lose something of value? Or what about when something doesn't live up to the hype of what you thought it would be? For many, it is an evolving series of emotional reactions that consistently weaves and worms its way towards depression. As we introduce our scripture reference for this matter, be mindful of your reactions to past losses and objectively ponder whether you are indeed still grasping onto the actual loss itself, or the feeling of the loss. While this may be interpreted as insensitive, I can assure you it is not. This realization was key for biblically grieving and accepting the loss of my mother and the eventual estrangement of my daughter.

For I know the plans I have for you, declares the Lord, plans for welfare and not for evil, to give you a future and a hope.

Jeremiah 29:11

In Jeremiah chapter 29, reference verses 4 through 14 for the full context, but I will provide a quick synopsis. Because of Israel's continued disobedience, they were taken captive by the Babylonians. God chose to speak to His people – through Jeremiah's writing – in a letter. God proceeds to tell them to continue living life; build houses, dwell in them, plant gardens, marry and have children. He also tells them to seek the welfare of the land they have been exiled to and pray for it. Because in doing so, they would find their welfare during captivity there.

They have lost loved ones, house and homes, land, temples, and their city. Adding insult to injury, God even tells them that this exile will last for over 70 years before He comes back to free them. Let that sink in; captive for 70 years, an entire generation would most likely come and go. Those who were originally taken captive would die as a refugee in a foreign land.

By all accounts, they have a right to be sad, to be depressed. How could God tell them to keep living life and act like nothing happened? This seems like such a peculiar and absurd statement. While God obviously knew the rest of the story, I acknowledge this instruction to be in direct response to our human propensity to hyper-focus on the circumstances, by associating overwhelming emotions and loss of eternal perspective. Notice He didn't tell them to give up or give in, He told them to keep living and go about a *good* routine. However, He didn't just leave it at that. He also gave them a promise. A promise we can also choose to believe or not. The same genus of choice we instinctively make when allowing ourselves to remain tyrannized by depression. But we must come to terms with the loss and realize it does not ultimately define us.

If we allow what we have lost to demarcate us, we will easily become enslaved in the routine of recycling feelings over and over again with the dawning of every new day. [This isn't to say that what is missing is not as compelling as what is present. However, this subject happens to be a specific instance of a general abstraction known as *negative space*. Similarly, a conversation can be had regarding the differences between negative consequences for poor behavior (naturally occurring and primal) and positive reinforcement for proper behavior (mindfully and logically chosen). In the same manner, this conceptual thought lies parallel to the understanding that darkness wasn't created, but rather is the absence of light. As St. Augustine noted (*privatio boni*), "Evil is the absence of good." It is simply not comprehensive enough to only acknowledge what is in absentia, we must intentionally appreciate what remains.]

BREAK THE ROUTINE

What happens when your morning routine is interfered with? Being a recovering addict, routines are easy enough to create just as long as it is an activity we are interested in or see as useful. We addicts are great at crafting routines and habits. For us though, the difference between success and failure at the things that matter in life, are the habits we choose. Bad ones aren't going to produce good outcomes, no matter how much we hope they will.

Granted, it is slightly easier to create a habit than to break one. Nonetheless, the insane amount of intentional commitment required to restrain from the familiar can be offset by choosing to invest in a new habit of routine. As much as depression is a habit, hope is as well. Hope requires us to not just solely focus on the good or the bad (as if they are the only possible recipients of our attention), but rather to fix our gaze upon God. This resistance to change (inertia) makes it vitally important to first begin by shifting our focus from the circumstances in our lives to better understanding the character of God. Circumstances will change, God doesn't. Breaking the agonizing pattern of depression requires us to do something different. Illuminating why depression is so magnetic, we don't *want* to do anything at all, let alone something different and potentially awkward.

Finally, brothers, whatever is true, whatever is honorable, whatever is just, whatever is pure, whatever is lovely, whatever is commendable, if there is any excellence, if there is anything worthy of praise, think about these things.

Philippians 4:8

Since there is far greater value in specifics than generalities, here are a few points to appraise and analyze. These are meant to spur active steps to break destructive habits of depression and institute new ones of hope. Feelings will fail you during the act of habit replacement. Therefore, make every effort to remain objective for the outcome instead of allowing these feelings to derail you. As His Word says, "He knows the plans He has for you." While we may not see the entirety of His plans, we can trust in Him because of His love for us.

1. Become self-aware of your habits.

   Slow down. Inquisitively and dynamically look at your life, from past to present. Look for the areas where justification appears to be prominent – making note of opinion and fact. Look for the times when emotions and feelings outweighed logic and discernment. Spiritual growth naturally catalyzes an increased self-awareness, which will distribute itself through our decisions and daily routines.

2. Break depression forming habits by replacing them with rewarding biblical ones.

   Sometimes, just making the effort is what counts, like going to the gym or dieting. Most people are not initially excited about the strain or hunger pains they perceive to be attributed. But eventually, days of hard work become weeks of commitment which turn into months of devotion, and they begin to experience positive results. It is the same with reading God's word. The twofold yield it produces is not only beneficial for ourselves but additionally for those around us. Remind yourself that this is an opportunity to explore something with an incomprehensible return on your investment.

3. Believe (not feel) there is something more.

   If Jesus decided to pay the debt we owed, then it draws the obvious conclusion that we are loved and cared for so much, that He willingly gave up His own life. That sacrificial act also communicates that we are worth more to Him than our debt. Because of this inherent value, we can cherish and believe that we were created for *something more* – but it will be up to you to find out:

   What is that something more?

Lynette Oliver

> "The grief I experienced when my son lost his life to an overdose was like a vacuum that created a void of complete darkness in my heart."

That darkness swallowed up my joy and peace – I felt lost. Addiction had already stolen so much from me. While other moms were swapping stories about their children's achievements and successes, I spent tearful days and sleepless nights praying my son would call; but being terrified that if the phone rang it would be the one call I didn't want.

Addiction stole everything it could and then took my child's life and suddenly while other moms were planning weddings or baby showers, I was planning a funeral. Mothers aren't supposed to have to live without their children. It's just not natural. Yet there I was trying to figure out how to live without my boy. The darkness consumed me, and I wasn't sure I would ever truly be able to see light again. I knew I would have to live with this pain forever, but I didn't want it to be in vain.

I cried out to God and asked Him to give my pain some purpose, to give me a reason to press on through the pain. God answered that prayer, and a ministry was born. Out of the dark void of my pain and grief, God created a beautiful purpose for my life by allowing me to help people struggling with addictions find and pay for rehab opportunities, coordinating support groups for families with addicted loved ones, hosting classes for those in recovery, meeting basic needs of those in our community experiencing homelessness and also employing recovering addicts.

I will never get over the death of my son, but God's love and the opportunity to use my experience to help others has allowed me to walk out of that consuming darkness of grief, and back into the light.

OVERCOME

PHILIPPIANS 1 6
JOHN 6 37
JOHN 14 18
1 PETER 2 11
MATTHEW 6 33
JEREMIAH 17 9
JOSHUA 1 9
JEREMIAH 29 11
GALATIANS 5 1
PROVERBS 11 2
MATTHEW 11 28
EPHESIANS 2 10
JEREMIAH
1 PETER 5 8
PSALM 147 3
MATTHEW 6 27
JOHN 16 33
ROMANS 12 2

IV

Burden and Comfort

LEGACY?

What are you working for and striving towards? What do you find yourself consistently investing in? What end result do you expect? These are questions many of us entertain but never really answer. As a result of neglecting this foresight, just getting through the day without the wheels falling off supplants thoughts of terms like *longevity* and *legacy*. These two concepts are often relegated to obscurity (since so few consider them), that unfortunately, more uncertainties exist regarding this subject than answers, depending on where you look.

If you could go back and choose any career path you wanted, what would it be? Is it different than what you are doing right now? For a select few, this may be a straightforward answer. But for the majority, our answers take a leisurely Sunday drive. Be that as it may, we are tied up in labor for most of our lives. When we came into this world, we were given a yoke – one that the world spends much of our lives adding to. We are burdened with an overcommitted schedule, domestic discord, continual struggle, temptations, accomplishment, and performance.

Regrettably, we typically identify with the sources of our burdens and struggles more so than asking the question "Why did we choose to struggle with this specific burden in the first place?" Is this baggage even something you are remotely interested in carrying around everywhere you go? Have you consciously strapped this burden to your back or is someone or something else responsible? These inquiries may not make very much sense presently, but I am confident by the end of this chapter the answers will disclose themselves rather freely.

You may be thinking that you are pretty content right now with no huge problems. While my intent is not to turn you into a neurotic, humor the attempt and let me pose a few further symptomatic questions. Do you find yourself spending sleepless nights deliberating the same issues? Do you feel exhausted most of the time? Do you have a lack of joy even when taking part in activities that you used to enjoy at one time? Has your Christian walk become a dried-up hobby? Have you lost interest?

The word *interest* is fairly, well... interesting. For the most part, it encompasses nouns like enthusiasm and curiosity. While financially, its language speaks in dividends and profits. The reason I want to fixate on this word directly is that Nikola Tesla once said, "the major difference between a genius and others is their imagination and level of interest." By all accounts, Tesla was considered a gifted man, many years before his time – like Leonardo Da Vinci was with mechanics, Tesla was with electricity.

Be that as it may, if you weren't gifted, then Malcolm Gladwell has stated that if you want to become what is designated as world-class in any field of your choosing, you must spend 10,000 deliberate hours practicing that discipline. (Mathematically, this equates to eight hours a day, five days a week for five years.) Not sure about you, but I'd rather have been gifted, such as Tesla and Da Vinci – albeit their giftedness was supplemented by spending way more than five years practicing their passions. I'm far too old and lazy to want to learn anything new, at least that is what the human side says. Nevertheless, it behooves us to ponder if we are indeed sacrificing for things we are interested in and see some sort of value for? If not, then where exactly are our efforts and resources going?

DUALITY

Are you aware that at this very moment, you have a yoke on your shoulders? We are all born with a yoke but, we also all have a choice of the yoke we wear. For some of us, this may come as news. Vulgar. Repulsive. News. We have an actual choice in life as to what yoke we put on every single day. One yoke will scheme to tear down, while the other attempts to build up. When you take one yoke off, the other one goes on. We will always wear a yoke in one manner or the other.

"Come to me, all you who are weary and burdened, and I will give you rest. Take my yoke upon you and learn from me, for I am gentle and humble in heart, and you will find rest for your souls. For my yoke is easy and my burden is light."

Matt 11:28-30 (NIV)

To best understand what Jesus is saying, it would befit us to become acquainted with some of the terms and their implication for our argument. A *yoke* is an apparatus that is hitched up to an animal to pull a load. It is a human invention to pull more, faster, further; not the design of the beast that is wearing it. The world's yoke is demanding and unforgiving, while the yoke of Jesus is forgiving and full of grace. One yoke tells you the grave is calling, and the hours are few. The other promises rest for your soul. Nonetheless, the yoke is a reminder to the one wearing it, that they are lumbering towards a destination.

A good way to know what yoke you have on is to look at what you are serving and sacrificing for. Where are your hours going to and for what purpose? This ultimately determines the burdens you carry and whether they are tearing you down or building you up. When I reached my nexus and hit rock bottom, I knew there was nowhere else to go. I found the end of myself and realized life could not go on any longer like this. It is here, that you begin to scratch the surface and find out what yoke you are truly wearing.

The word *burdened* (or 'heavy laden' depending on your translation) means to be overloaded. It describes a heavy heart; one beaten down, calloused, jaded, and tormented. Figuratively, burden can be pictured as a rickety wooden wagon hauling around and collecting worries, unmet demands, unconfessed and unrepentant sin, and broken dreams. Hopefully, we figure out what the maximum load limit is before we break the axles or die of dysentery. (This analogy was brought to you by *Oregon Trail*, the only reason elementary school existed back in the 1980s.)

Next, the word *weary*. Weary is a poetic way of saying tired or worn out. Weary is the feeling that comes from being burdened. And yes, it is highly plausible to become weary even while doing good things. Demonstrably, God's word is fully aware of this phenomenon:

And let us not grow weary of doing good, for in due season we will reap, if we do not give up.

Galatians 6:9

And finally, the word *rest*. Rest conjures up notions of renewal and reinvigoration in the mental, physical, emotional, and spiritual departments. At times, you may just need a nap, some fresh air, maybe a vacation and some sunshine, or a cheeseburger. But for this context, the word rest distinctly implies spiritual rest – a lack of turmoil and a surplus of rejuvenation. Jesus continually signals toward the fact that the here and now has an impact on the ever after. Since we humans are not *either-or* creations (either human or spiritual), we illogically tend to adopt a mistaken perspective regarding our existence. We are in fact *both-and* creatures – exhibiting the duality of the physical and the spiritual – each one perfectly capable of affecting and disrupting the other.

Since burdens are an ever-present part of life, I have had to ask God to please renew me through the adversities and the relentless sources of demand, instead of removing them. (Selfishly, my prayer used to be for Him to eliminate the constant requests from others. But when my many petitions were not answered, I found myself resentful and ironically burdened because I felt compelled to help others, assuming I had no choice in the matter.) Since attempting to adopt and instill this shift of perspective, burdens are now beginning to transform from coincidental impositions and annoyances to purposeful appointments and opportunities.

EXCHANGE
And here is where we find the main takeaway from our discussion – the exchanging of yokes. As stated previously, some burdens debilitate us, while others strengthen us, but an exchange will always occur. Being a Christ-follower, we are equipped with faith – the unique and potential ability to shift our perspective from temporarily physical to eternally spiritual, by applying the truth of the gospel. This faith allows us to pause for a moment and accept there is a spiritual and eternal reason for the burden.

In exploring this concept, suppose the probability of sustaining an extensive and total lifestyle change in two separate scenarios. In the first example, what would you predict the chances of success to be when attempting to massively alter or adopt a complete lifestyle change *without* God at the very center – 100%, 50%, 1%?

In the second scenario, suppose that the very Creator of the universe is at the helm of the ship, and we are not interfering with the sails or trying to snatch the wheel out of His hand (instead we are more than likely in the background swabbing the poop deck or something nautical sounding like that). Would you predict the chance of success to be any better or worse than the first example? Common sense tells me that He knows where we are going, I don't. I do not know the seas or the winds, what to do when a rogue wave appears, or how to handle the Kraken that has been pursuing us since we left port – He does.

To bring this concept down to a hands-on applicable level, I encourage you to take part in the following experiment.

Exchange one burden that is tearing you down for one that will build you up.

While you are giving up ownership of it, you will need to find something to exchange it for to fill the empty space it has left, but it must be something that will build you up. For example, trade watching television in the evening for studying Proverbs. Or perhaps exchange smoking for starting and maintaining a prayer journal. The proposition is to focus on a substantial purpose during this exchange. When you feel the desire to put the yoke of destructive burden on, actively choose to leave it in the closet and at least try on the restorative yoke of Jesus for a change of pace.

Kevin Varble

> "I battled with not feeling worthy or good enough for most of my life."

I lived a fairly successful life, I was that guy that friends and family would come to for support, but the truth was I was hiding from so many addictions. It wasn't until July 7, 2016, that my life would take a turn that no one saw coming. That was the first time I did Meth and it changed my life forever. That drug brought me to my lowest and it exposed all the sins I had been hiding from for years – the depression, porn, sexual, brokenness, anger, and drug addiction. Little did I know at that time God was breaking my legs because I had been running and trying to hide from Him for so long.

It wasn't until I hit my rock bottom and found myself in jail for a third time in a week, that I knew I needed something better. But from all the heavy drug use and my very selfish ways, I still had this "yeah, right" attitude when I was released. I knew I needed God's help but I didn't know how or what to do – I had burnt every bridge, and no one was going to help, or so I thought. It wasn't until I walked into a meeting and met my now good friend Ron, that I felt there was hope.

I spent another few months still trying to do it my way but it wasn't working. I finally surrendered and after four and a half months, God led me to a ministry that helped men develop a relationship with Christ.

Even though I still fought Him to do things my way, He had bigger and better plans for me. But first, we had some work to do, painful work that felt like He was pruning me with a chainsaw. I started laying everything at His feet and He started changing me. He started using me and man, did that get scary because I started feeling peace; something I had never felt before. God had started turning my life around because it was no longer about me, it became all about Him and serving others, just as he has led me to do.

Today, I still have to give it all to Him every single day and that struggle is real. BUT GOD!!! He is using me in ways I could have never thought of. I now work at an addiction ministry where I get to help men and women get their lives back together and talk about Jesus all day and that is truly a blessing! So, when times get tough, always remember:

Be still and know that I am God.

Psalm 46:10a

OVERCOME

PHILIPPIANS 1 6

JOHN 14 18

JEREMIAH 17 9

JOHN 6 37

JOSHUA 1 9

JEREMIAH 29 11

GALATIANS 5 1

PROVERBS 11 2

MATTHEW 11 28

1 PETER 2 10

MATTHEW 6 33

EPHESIANS 2 10

1 PETER 5 8

PSALM 147 3

MATTHEW 6 27

JOHN 16 33

ROMANS 12 2

V

Trauma and Healing

BATTLEFIELD TRIAGE

Whether from our environment or self-induced, traumatic events can often consume us. Bitterness, anger, and depression are commonly grafted into our lives from these events; and when we have not adequately grieved and healed, these wounds grow deeper and become acutely infected and sensitive to the touch. Without proper care, these injuries then decay us from the inside out, and we set up permanent residence there when it was only supposed to be a rental for the weekend.

Without properly attending to wounds, we humans normally resort to performing something known as *battlefield triage*. But without correctly diagnosing, we just apply a tourniquet. Back in the days of the civil war, before antibiotics and most medical advancements, the treatment for some severe enough wounds was to sever the infected limb off, cauterize the stump shut with a hot iron, and employ leaches for subcutaneous hematoma (a result of the swelling and bruising caused by the injury and surgery).

Agonizingly though, many of these antiquated dismemberments could have been prevented in retrospect. Since the practitioners of old possessed few of our modern medical procedures, many amputations (and even deaths) occurred due to unsterilized equipment and barbaric hack-

and-slash surgical method, which usually led to unnecessary infections, additional surgeries, and repetitious application of anesthesia (by the way, the 'knock em out juice' for civil war era tent surgeons was chloroform. Overexposure to this specific chemical frequently led to coma and, morbidly ironic, death). It was a roll of the dice if you survived the injury – let alone surgery – but an almost grim certainty if you did nothing at all to treat the wound.

If you grew up in the southern United States, you have likely heard your fair share of crazy old-timers' cures. Cigar smoke in your ear to cure aches or drinking a tea made from rabbit dung to fix up a hangover (alcoholics who partook in this remedy also coincidentally developed chronic halitosis for some odd reason). While comical and rather absurd, many people still prescribe to this sort of 'where there's a will there's a way' doctrine today.

For example, the *placebo effect* is a psychological term that basically means if you give enough credence to a treatment, it will work. Medical science has confirmed this oddity through clinical trials where one group of people are given an activated medication. Another group, the control, is given a dummy pill, usually containing a basic starch, called a placebo. The first group that received the real medication is queried regarding their experience, as well as the group that received the fake medication. Surprisingly, in all these trials, a percentage of the placebo control group mysteriously reports experiencing some sort of effect. Whether this occurs due to the power of outside suggestion or self-based deception, science cannot authenticate. Regardless, it has been empirically observed and proven to occur time and again, in various trials.

Now, don't get me wrong, there are certain underlying attributes to support some of these old-timer's cures, like the use of aloe on a burn or the credible utility of castor oil (how someone discovered it was specifically useful as a laxative is a dreadful discussion for another time). Capitalistically though, an entire industry sprang up in the 1800s that relied upon and exploited this sort of placebo group think: snake oil elixirs, which owes much of its success to something called the power of suggestion.

For many of us, when we first hear the ideas of the previous centuries, they seem archaic and outdated. We, of course, are so much more enlightened and dignified, right? Regardless of however facetiously worded the previous sentence, the very same thing occurs today. Many medications prescribed in our day and time do not authentically address the illness but instead create just enough side effects to mask and distract the afflicted from the symptoms they are enduring. Lending further credence to the suspicion that there is no money in a cure...

BITTER MEDICINE
Before we go any further, please bear in mind, this perspective is meant to educate and encourage. Trauma is a titanic thesis to unpack (in so few words), and I want to be as calculated as possible. Since dealing with distress feels like chasing phantoms, it makes logical sense to begin our case by looking at what induces trauma and alternately, what trauma produces in the same breath. Much of the production and reaction to trauma are tied together and cannot be easily untangled and separated into neat little threads once you start unraveling it all.

Overarchingly, trauma is a direct result of what others have done to us and what our reaction is to the offense; with the major variables being the severity of the damage and time required for healing. For many of us, we are victims of generational trauma that has rippled throughout our family tree. We find ourselves repeating many of the same actions we have seen (good or bad) and spend many years ironing out wrinkled-up dilemmas our parents and grandparents have tried to wad up and cram in a dresser drawer. 'Who needs enemies when you have family' cynically finds perfect usage when discussing generational baggage. Although familial concerns are a large producer of trauma, they are not the only origin. Trauma can occur anywhere and anytime.

Simply put, words and actions provoke trauma; a careless word spoken in the heat of an argument or an action by a loved one. We witness and experience these events, interpreting and subconsciously assigning a value to them. It naturally becomes a subject of thought and eventually forms a memory we stow away and forget about; soon directing how we see and live life. When this occurs, we become desensitized to the effects of those words and actions, thereby expediting the cycle of devastation. This cycle will ultimately dictate if, and to what degree, we become instigators of future traumatic events or remain in an arrested state of development, traceable back to these past experiences we have buried deep down inside.

There is one suggested caveat to this discussion, though. If you find yourself in the valley of processing a traumatic event, contact a counselor or find a fellow believer and speak with them. It may take some time to locate the right one but look for one who will walk with you during this time, especially if you are in the early stages of recovery. When an individual is in the midst of addiction that is also suffering from past traumatic events, the natural inclination is to hunt for something that will distract, medicate, numb, or kill the pain. Without consciously recognizing it, we are advocating on behalf of the snake oil theory, no matter how little it does or how bitter the taste is.

SCAR TISSUE

In Psalms, we will find another promise from God's word. Cut a major artery and they tell you to remain calm. Why? Because the more frantic we get, the faster our heart pumps. The quicker our pulse, the greater the volume of blood we are going to lose. In the same manner, with the following verse, we need to slow down and pause. This can be done by intentionally forming a picture in our mind. Imagine you have been injured – any severe wound. This will act as a visual analog for a traumatic event we will use to explore for the duration of this chapter.

He heals the brokenhearted and binds up their wounds.

Psalm 147:3

Our reaction to this traumatic event will obviously motivate our next decision: how are we going to handle it? Bacteria are often introduced when wounds occur. Therefore, we can suppose that the wound will likely become infected, leading to many painful long-term difficulties. Physiologically, the body responds to irritants and foreign matter with a ramping up of white blood cell production – which fights off the pathogens that have found a way in. Spiritually, when trauma is mishandled, sores are created within our souls, acting as sites for infiltrating the host with illnesses (such as unforgiveness) and eventually gatecrashes every nook and cranny of life. Our spiritual defenses must be inoculated regularly with an infusion of the gospel truth – the only way to sustain the reparative healing process. A placebo will just not suffice.

As time passes, these wounds will heal and become something more resilient than before. Recently I read a quote that said the skill and precision of a surgeon can be ascertained by the proportion of scar tissue that forms during the healing process. What this means is an excellent surgeon could make a wound virtually disappear, within reason. For followers of Christ, we have access to a much greater Surgeon that will not only heal our wounds but make them a source of unique strength.

CONNECT THE DOTS

Presently, if you find yourself entangled in a traumatic event, all that this type of healing requires to begin is a choice. Albeit, if the event is hidden behind some sort of mental fog, we are compelled to consciously begin looking at current actions and feelings to see how they may be connected to past events. For me, this was done with a notebook and solitude. You will be looking for evidence, the existence of any dots that may be fully or partially responsible for behaviors and reactions you can trace back. In many cases, they are so deeply rooted, that we are subconsciously led and directed by them throughout the day, without ever truly being aware of what is genuinely pulling our strings.

As you are made aware of these events you must then take them to God to get His perspective on them. Doing this will help begin the process by recognizing our reactions to past traumatic events. This isn't done to criminalize the victim or lessen the pain by discrediting the suffering of the account. It is to accept that the trauma has occurred and allows the gospel to heal in such a way that we are no longer defined by our scars, but rather by the skill of the Surgeon.

While vexatious and irritating, we must come to terms and realize we live in a fallen world; unpleasant and downright revolting events are going to occur. Sin leads to suffering and we humans are a chaotically sinful species. We hurt people we don't know, and they hurt us. Most damaging though, is the consistent – and habitually convenient – harm caused by (and to) those closest to each other. This type of familiar wound isn't so much physical, as it is mental and emotional – the injuries we can't see – the *brokenhearted*.

DISCHARGE

An uncomplicated choice (and possibly the most grotesque one you may ever make) will reveal itself when you realize there is a treatment option that can and will heal this infectious, traumatic wound: the choice to forgive. This choice isn't just a suggestion either – God tells us to forgive – and it will take trust in Him to do it. Forgiving another person who has harmed you, especially when in such close proximity, is a lasting antiseptic for the soul. Much like iodine, it will sting at first, and possibly for a long time, depending on how infected the injury is. But the fact that God offers forgiveness to us is clearly evidenced throughout the bulk of the Bible as an ever-present theme.

SPECIMEN #1

Be kind to one another, tenderhearted, forgiving one another, as God in Christ forgave you.

Ephesians 4:32

SPECIMEN #2

---

bearing with one another and, if one has a complaint against another, forgiving each other; as the Lord has forgiven you, so you also must forgive.

Col 3:13

SPECIMEN #3

And Jesus said, "Father, forgive them, for they know
not what they do."

Luke 23:34a

We are told to forgive because it is for our good.
Forgiveness is choosing to no longer let the wound impair
your life. Making this choice does not require you to think,
feel, or believe that the other person deserves forgiveness.
Nor does it matter if they have apologized or even asked you
to forgive them. Understandably, since this appears to be
relatively counter-intuitive, take a moment to internalize in
your heart what you are about to read next...

Forgiveness is not for the other persons' benefit. It is for your good.

Understand, I am not trying to sell you a magic potion that
will 'cure what ails ya'. It is not going to fix male pattern
baldness, acne, or gout. It does however heal your heart and
soul. Forgiving those who seriously injured me in the past
has been a core catalyst for spiritual growth, freedom, and
joy. If you suspect you may be suffering from the effects of
unforgiveness, I encourage you to make this a priority and
invest some time searching your heart. If you harbor any
unforgiveness, at least entertain the thought of giving up the
debt they owe you. Because the truth is, they can't pay it
back or even make it up, no matter how hard they try. Their
attempts are not going to pick up the broken pieces and put
them back together again. The love of God is what heals and
makes us whole.

Diane Hendrickson

"For many years, drug addiction ruined my life, and I wasn't even the one using them."

My experience with addiction is tragic, and like a train wreck, the devastation was complete. I lost my son, my only child, to a meth addiction that warped his mind, and ultimately convinced him the only way out was suicide. In all honesty, finding the redemptive power of God in this situation is like trying to see without my glasses. Try as I might, I have to squint and strain to catch a glimpse of it. In the natural, it eludes me. Without intention and effort, I am nearly blind to it.

Not long after my son's death, I realized I had an opportunity to choose. I could choose the easy route, to stay in my silo of isolation and despair, or I could take God at His word and move forward. I could choose to turn one tragedy into two or to believe that God means what He says in His word, that He loves me. That He works all things together for my good because I love Him. That He knows what is best for me because He is God, and I am not. Every day, I need to put on my corrective lenses in order to see clearly with my physical eyes. It's no different for me spiritually.

To see the redemptive power of God in this situation, I must view my experience with addiction through the corrective lenses of gratitude. While I will never be thankful that my son is dead, I can choose to be thankful he is no longer suffering in the hell of addiction here and is in heaven now.

It is not uncommon for me to question God when I'm feeling particularly frustrated that things did not turn out the way I planned. "Why, God?" The answer is free will. I can shake my fist at the sky or be thankful He did not create us to be puppets. At least initially, my son chose a path. Despite and through it all, I will put on my lenses of gratitude, and choose mine.

OVERCOME

JOHN 6 37

PHILIPPIANS 1 6

JOHN 6 27

JOHN 14 18

1 PETER 2 11

MATTHEW 6 33

JEREMIAH 17 9

JOSHUA 1 9

JEREMIAH 29 11

GALATIANS 5 1

PROVERBS 11 2

MATTHEW 11 28

EPHESIANS 2 10

1 PETER 5 8

PSALM 147 3

MATTHEW 6 27

JOHN 16 33

ROMANS 12 2

VI

Anxiety and Confidence

YOUR OWN PERSONAL GOLIATH

Worry, doubt, panic, distress; symptoms all brought on by stressful situations. Whether factual or fabricated, these episodes can have physical effects on our bodies, not just our minds. Thoughts do in fact have power and reveal their strength in the form of a debilitating paralysis that is often accompanied by requests to self-medicate. But, in the grand scheme of things, maybe we should assess what exactly it is that we are getting from all this worry in the first place. Anxiety is a clunky matter to define in origin and the many avenues it travels, so in efforts to flatten out the creases, let's get an opening statement on the floor before we go any further.

I worry about _____ too often.

What does anxiety look like for you? For me, anxiety is the imagination running wild – fearing the outcome and possible punishments and repercussions from past decisions. But in the cluttered mess of the anxious mind, the probability of everything becoming a colossal goat rope is always high. Many times, we are vulnerable to this state of mind as soon as we wake up in the morning. And since we don't typically expect positive things to happen, we worry and lose any form of peace we had even if the day is a magnificent specimen of fortune and favor. This loss of assurance is directly related to our lack of trust in God. Those of us who suffer from anxiety are not only damaging to ourselves but are highly contagious (and gratingly troublesome) to others by stealing joy and confidence through unintendedly planting seeds of doubt during our frantic episodes.

Anxiety – loss of control, holding our breath, waiting for the other shoe to drop – all add to the feeling of bearing the weight of the world on your shoulders. We just can't help ourselves and eventually we buckle under the self-imposed pressure. Everything is urgent and requires immediate attention. The only way we know how to deal with this is to either become obnoxiously overbearing and micro-manage every aspect or escape and find something to take the edge off. These *escapes* come in various forms of distractions and destructive misconduct. When we fail to promptly deal with legitimate issues, our hypersensitivity to the 'what-ifs' quickly exceeds an acceptable level of operational worry. No longer manageable, it starts to manifest physically within us and spills out over the edge.

AN ANALOGY
Open your bible to 1 Samuel 17. We are going to look at one of the more famous altercations in the Bible. In this story, we have a scene that has developed, and we will draw a parallel to a few details in it, as it relates to our focus.

Goliath was a Philistine champion, who was a monstrous man and a massive problem for the Israelites. He intimidated them and contested them. In his challenge, he gave them a reward for victory and a penalty for defeat. Over the course of forty days, he continued to taunt and bully them, but the Israelites were afraid and would not respond. That is until a little boy named David approached the king with a liberating proposal. Keep this scenario in mind for a moment and bookmark your Bible. We will be returning to it shortly.

ORIGIN
Now, flip to Matthew, the first book of the New Testament. The Sermon on the Mount starts in chapter 5 and proceeds through chapter 7. In this sermon, Jesus will teach about anger, lust, prayer, money, criticizing others, and much more. The specific section we are going to look at happens almost directly in the middle of the sermon.

And which of you by being anxious can add a single hour to his span of life?

Matt 6:27

For this verse of scripture, a study on the word *anxious* may prove to be the most fruitful as we begin. In the King James Version, the phrase *taking thought* is used instead of the word anxious. If we go to Strong's Concordance and trace back the phrase 'taking thought' to its etymological origin, we get many words that allude to the conceptual idea of being distracted because of doubt. The way I interpret this verse is simply that worrying will not provide anything useful, nor is it going to help our cause. Worry, and more precisely the outcome of worry provides no value – in any way, shape, or form. Worry distracts us from the reality of the situation.

It is rudimental and lazy to tell someone, "Don't worry" because it is not an acceptable replacement for suitable advice. In response to this negligence, once we get to the application for this chapter, we are going to have an actual project to take part in and use as a magnifying glass to discern if our worrying is even justified or just a monumental waste of time.

For our discussion, please extend the courtesy of allowing the premise to exist (if but for the duration of this chapter) that anxiety and confidence could possibly just be habits we find ourselves returning to; like a rhythm or the cadence a metronome clicks to. I do not ask you to blindly believe this hypothesis; but for a few moments, simply allow it to exist while we are unpacking this topic. Because overarchingly, the contrast between anxiety and confidence dwells within the realm of trust and responsibility. As well, in hopes of being as comprehensive as possible, I would be a careless detective if I didn't at least acknowledge there is also a possible measure of patent anxiety bred into us from our original mother and father way back in the garden.

And they heard the sound of the Lord God walking in the garden in the cool of the day, and the man and his wife hid themselves from the presence of the Lord God among the trees of the garden. But the Lord God called to the man and said to him, "Where are you?" And he said, "I heard the sound of you in the garden, and I was afraid, because I was naked, and I hid myself."

Genesis 3:8-10

We are not strangers to the riotous maelstrom that anxiety incites within us. Some people are naturally laid back and easygoing, while others get readily wrapped up in concerning and negative thoughts. As stated previously, having suffered from panic attacks in the past, they were usually set in motion from some random concern that grew way out of proportion and escaped cranial confinement. And before you knew it, everything had imploded and collapsed in on itself. Your heart raced, you hyper-ventilated and nothing seemed to pacify. For a long period of time, I self-medicated to cope with anxiety and used addiction to hide from worry, the same way Adam and Eve did with God. All because I didn't trust Him, and knew I had done wrong.

---

do not be anxious about anything, but in everything by prayer and supplication with thanksgiving let your requests be made known to God. And the peace of God, which surpasses all understanding, will guard your hearts and your minds in Christ Jesus.

Philippians 4:6-7

Do you trust God in all things? Do you trust God to keep the sun shining, to keep the Earth spinning, to wake you in the morning and furnish another breath in your lungs after the previous one has vacated? Do you trust Jesus when He said He was leaving for a time to prepare a new home for us? Do you trust God with the big stuff like keeping this blue and green marble floating and rotating in the nothingness of space? If so, then doesn't it logically conclude that we would have confidence that He is looking out for us in even the most minuscule areas of life as well?

DIVIDE AND CONQUER

Grab a piece of paper and draw a crosshair shape, like so **+**. But draw it as big as you can. This will act as a visual layout for the logical assessment we are going to conduct. As strange as it may sound, we are going to use this little graph to diagnose anxiety and provide a treatment plan. These four panes will represent a unique window we will use to sift our concerns with. For each quadrant, there will be a specific label, a few questions, and a little applicable insight to guide you through the rest of this cataloging exercise. Begin by listing out and organizing these concerns into the following categories.

1.   *(Top Left)*

     CONCERNS YOU ARE NOT RESPONSIBLE FOR

     Is this something I am liable for, or is this another person's responsibility and something outside of my control? You can be burdened for what someone else is doing with their life, but ultimately their decisions are between them and God. Make every effort to not allow these concerns to consume you.

2.   *(Top Right)*

     CONCERNS THAT MAY NOT EVEN BE POSSIBLE

     Is what I am worried about even a possibility? This is typically determined to be *invalid* in the world of logic. "There is a 1 in 297,400,000 chance I *could* win the lottery…"

3.   *(Bottom Left)*

     CONCERNS YOU ARE DIRECTLY RESPONSIBLE FOR

     Is this something I am responsible for? Am I doing things that are actively increasing my level of anxiety: poor financial choices, known and habitual sin? (Spoiler alert - this is going to be one category of focus…)

4.   *(Bottom Right)*

     CONCERNS THAT ARE LIKELY PROBABLE

     Is this worry probable? In logic, this is known as *valid*. "…but it's not probable that I *would* win the lottery." (…and this will be the other category.)

For example:

1
are not responsible for

how your neighbor's dog behaves

2
may not even be possible

asteroid hitting the earth,
creating a zombie apocalypse

3
are directly responsible for

bills are late again

4
are likely probable

car might get repo'd next time

Use this tool to logically determine if your concerns are within your control and probable. Or are they only possible and the responsibility falls on another person. This isn't to shirk your responsibility, but to help empower you to address what you are capable of addressing and letting go of things you cannot control. As instances fall into the bottom categories, 3 - concerns you are directly responsible for and 4 - concerns that are likely probable, make sure to prioritize them over the other two categories. If worries fall north of the equator line, congratulations. There is nothing you can do about them; they belong to God. You can be aware of them but realize you are not accountable for them. Every step you take forward will build confidence and ultimately help free you from the prison of anxiety.

TRUE YOUR AIM

In closing out this chapter, we will finish up the story we began with in 1 Samuel. Are your concerns probable and valid? Is it a 'Goliath' you have helped created and need to take some steps to address? Do you need to confess and repent from those decisions? If yes, then stop letting them taunt you and act as David did in the upcoming verses. An army of grown men cowered to Goliath, but David's confidence in God allowed him to step with a singularity of mission with no hesitation or distraction.

When the Philistine arose and came and drew near to meet David, David ran quickly toward the battle line to meet the Philistine. And David put his hand in his bag and took out a stone and slung it and struck the Philistine on his forehead. The stone sank into his forehead, and he fell on his face to the ground.

1 Samuel 17:48-49

Brooks Lancaster

> "My entire life was not always spent as a healthy walk with the Lord Jesus Christ."

For many years, in fact, I did quite the opposite; I ran from the love of the Father as hard as I could. Until one day I had lost everything and had come to a point where He was my only way out. What you are about to read is a quick story of my adventure into the bowels of addiction, how it took everything I had, and how I managed to escape to the other side as a better person. I write this with the hope that it brings exactly that into the life of those who may still be struggling with this in their own lives.

I began smoking cigarettes at an early age, then quickly progressed to marijuana, then alcohol shortly thereafter. I seemed to just do okay as a student where I cared far too much about having fun and getting with girls and not so much about my schoolwork. I was having sex on a weekly basis and living outside the will of God. Then one night after a ballgame I made a profession of faith, but the way I was living was not that of a young Christian man. I was living a lie and I didn't care who I was going to hurt. My drinking became more and more of a problem after high school until it led to a breakup with my high school sweetheart. The girl I thought I would marry.

My relationship with Christ became non-existent. I literally felt as if my world was going to collapse. This was when some "friends" introduced me to the new love of my life, one I would keep around for nearly fifteen years; her name was "Crystal" or crystal meth. With this now in my life, I felt as if I could conquer the world. There was no more pain, guilt, or suffering. Or so I thought till the day I finally ran out.

Things came to a screeching halt when I finally ran out of money and ran out of drugs. I had been involved in one failed relationship after another and had abused and betrayed everyone that ever genuinely cared about me. There was no use trying to find a legitimate job because selling dope was so much easier. That is until the legal walls began closing in on me. The only hope I had left was in the fact that I thought I was ready to take my own life, but something or someone stopped me. It was a still small voice telling me "I'm not through with you, get up, you still have work to do." I knew this was Jesus giving me the motivation to take back my life, but only through His redeeming grace.

That day I accepted Christ back into my life as Lord and Savior. I now allow Him to shepherd me each day as He continuously leads me back into the fold. He has restored all that was lost, and constantly gives me more than I deserve. He guides and directs me according to His perfect will for my life. On the three-year anniversary of my clean date, I was graciously accepted by my congregation and ordained as Deacon at Mud Creek Baptist Church where I will joyfully and faithfully serve Jesus' bride in whatever capacity I am called. The opportunity came in the Summer of 2017 to give back by taking a position as Men's placement coordinator with First Contact addiction Ministries, giving me a chance to tell my story on a daily basis with those who are trying to escape the bondage of addiction. My life is now a far cry from where it once was, but it is only because we have a God who loves us enough not to leave us dead in our sins.

OVERCOME

PHILIPPIANS 1 6

JOHN 14 18

JEREMIAH 17 9

JOSHUA 1 9

JOHN 6 37

1 PETER 2 11

MATTHEW 6 33

JEREMIAH 29 11

GALATIANS 5 1

PROVERBS 11 2

MATTHEW 11 28

EPHESIANS 2 10

1 PETER 5 8

PSALM 147 3

MATTHEW 6 27

JOHN 16 33

ROMANS 12 2

VII

Exhaustion and Renewal

MARKET SATURATION

This life is not easy. Period. We constantly fight – tooth and nail – just to scrape by. We rely on janky tools given to us by this world to obtain the treasures commercials flaunt nonstop on our screens. Relying on our own strength, we will only get so far in life, eventually paying a price we are just not prepared to pay.

We are all familiar with advertisements and how they manipulate us, right? Like this, follow them, buy this, eat that, wear this, listen up, watch this, date her, date him, work here, drive this, vote for, accept this, ignore that, be this person, hate that person, this will make you popular. *But wait there's more!* TV, movies, music, social media, check-out lines in the grocery store, shopping, and credit cards. We are saturated with a world that encourages conformity. Conformity that is demonstrated by the need to feel accepted and substantiated by our passive dependence on others to make decisions for us. This want to fit in is accomplished through imitation, compliance, identification, indoctrination, and internalization.

Thankfully though, a certain level of conformed manners is required and expected in social contexts. For example, wearing clothes, using the bathroom instead of the filing cabinet at work, personal hygiene such as deodorant and toothpaste are all part of a silent social contract most of us have no problem agreeing with. Assuming most of us have signed that contract and largely haven't been raised by wild wolves, we should now be able to graduate our investigation. In this chapter, we will address and arterially expose the fruitless search for fulfillment and the toll it takes on us through physical, mental, emotional, and spiritual exhaustion – the aftermath of striving to be accepted by the exclusive and all too elusive 'beautiful people.'

THE FIRST COMMERCIAL

From my studies in marketing, there are only two rules; (1) create the demand, and (2) supply the solution. The demand is created by attacking our identity and sowing doubt. Plain and simple. Make it appear to be a need, even though the consumer may not have been aware it was something they were without. Regardless of how attractive or exquisitely worded the campaign, step one principally insinuates:

> "Something is wrong with you. You are less than everyone else."

Marketing professionals know that the first step needs to be effective in order for the entire venture to be successful. If it is potent enough, all that is required for the second step then is to heroically supply the solution – by maliciously appealing to the doubt they just created a few moments earlier. It doesn't even need to make logical sense; it just needs to conclude by stating:

> "Luckily, we happen to have what will make you better. You are welcome."

Brilliant, right? Great advertisers know they want the consumer to buy into the ideology of the product, not its functionality. Most of the dogmatic narrative you see in advertising is used to this end, despite the nobility of the cause. The world is a master at deceptively propagating herd mentality, and we must be aware of it if we are going to combat it spiritually.

After doing some research, I found the very first sales pitch, and astoundingly it was in the first book of the Bible. Verses one through three capture the creation of the demand, while the next three verses supply the solution.

Now the serpent was more crafty than any other beast of the field that the Lord God had made. He said to the woman, "Did God say, 'You shall not eat of any tree in the garden'?" And the woman said to the serpent, "We may eat of the fruit of the trees in the garden, but God said, 'You shall not eat of the fruit of the tree that is in the midst of the garden, neither shall you touch it, lest you die.'

But the serpent said to the woman, "You will not surely die. For God knows that when you eat of it your eyes will be opened, and you will be like God, knowing good and evil." So when the woman saw that the tree was good for food, and that it was a delight to the eyes, and that the tree was to be desired to make one wise, she took of its fruit and ate, and she also gave some to her husband who was with her, and he ate.

Genesis 3:1-6

Face it, most of us are exhausted. For some right now, the suffering they are being forced to endure has depleted them. For others, it may be withering patience in dealing with challenging people and personality types or it may be a perpetually negative environment, littered with snares. In one shape or another, these trials are descriptive of the road we are traveling on through the stages of recovery.

DO NOT BE CONFORMED

Our anchor scripture comes from chapter 12 of the book of Romans. I refer to this section as 'You're a Christ-follower, now what do you do?' This scripture has three very distinct components. The first one obviously addresses conformity, while the second section provides the replacement activity by allowing yourself to be transformed. And finally, the reason (reward) is understood to be for your good.

Do not be conformed to this world, but be transformed by the renewal of your mind, that by testing you may discern what is the will of God, what is good and acceptable and perfect.

Romans 12:2

Conform is a verb that materially means to agree with or be similar to. It is the idea of being joined together and identifying with, by passive submission. The first portion of this verse is instructing us to not look like, think like, act like, or desire to be reflective of the world. Because when we do, we increase the likelihood of desensitization to certain issues via indoctrination – accepting something as the status quo without ever questioning it – because it envelopes us everywhere we go. We agree with what the world says about a particular grievance and adopt its perspective stance on it without looking to God and asking Him what His thoughts are on the matter. Worse yet, we do ask God for His input, then turn a deaf ear. Conformity advertises much but never delivers, leaving you always craving more. (P.T. Barnum popularized this "Always leave 'em wanting more" approach during his days with the circus. Which would explain the easy manipulation of our want-what-we-can't-have languishing and longing.) Miserably, we want the deception to be true because our identity and happiness hinge so desperately upon it becoming a factual condition of life.

The ramifications of worldly conformity result in working 90-hour weeks, absenteeism from your family, and turning to a wide selection of vices and distractions to fill the emptiness the chase has left you with. Conforming leads to medicating the disappointment and inadvertently instilling value systems in those around you that demonstrate to them that this *pursuit* is what life is really all about. We show them that constant exhaustion and disappointment are worth the price we pay. Since it is not, we seek material substance and experiences to fill the void, and during this journey, we subliminally believe the chase will somehow validate our life. This is what Paul is warning us against; the spiritual cost of conformity resulting in buyer's remorse.

BE TRANSFORMED

But in order to be transformed by the renewal of our mind, we would do well to work out a few particulars. Over the years, I have learned that if I can achieve mental agreeance with something, it will usually be adopted into my value system. While this isn't always the case with every matter, I do believe that when God pulls back the curtain and gives you a glimpse of something divine, you better take it to heart. To *be transformed* insinuates a dramatic change. The best way to fully grasp this word is to look at the roots of the word itself. *Transform* is a portmanteau (formed by combing two or more different words together). In this case, the first word *trans*, means across, beyond, or through. When the second-word *form* is added, it takes on the meaning of a change in shape, focus, direction. The word 'transform' originates from another portmanteau. The Greek word *meta* – transcendently taking on a form that embodies an inner essence – and *morpho* – to change after being with. This is where we get the word *metamorphosis* from. Just think of the change a caterpillar undergoes when springtime comes.

To be transformed means not only our appearance but our inner essence and beliefs have dramatically and markedly changed. If our beliefs change, then our thoughts change, our value systems change, and ultimately our actions change. We are not talking about an improvement, but rather, the creation of something entirely new. We exchange our thoughts and the world's conformity for God's thoughts and renewal. We are renewed by meditating and dwelling on God's almighty word. Coming into contact with Gods' word will always elicit a response; rejection or transformation. That is how powerful it is.

Behold, I am doing a new thing;

Isaiah 43:19a

FOR YOUR GOOD

For a long time, I viewed God as this cosmic killjoy, playing chess in the heavens, who took great pleasure in preventing good things from happening in my life, while directing torment my way. This immaturity affected my beliefs, which in turn publicized themselves through my actions. It was only after many tantrums in my early days of recovery and faith, did I even remotely begin to grasp the notion that there was a slight chance I didn't have a clue what I was doing, let alone what was actually good for me. I did not realize God loved me all those years previously, that He was trying to protect me, but I just wouldn't accept it.

God loves you, whether you excel or fail. If He didn't, I'm convinced He wouldn't have sent His Son to come to Earth and die by crucifixion. With that knowledge, we will conclude with the third major element of this scripture; *for your good*.

The truth of the matter is only God knows what is good for us. And as much as we want to think otherwise, we don't have a clue. The same way the serpent advertised the tree in the garden of Eden, we have accepted what the world advertises. Even in the midst of God giving Adam and Eve free will and choice, He was also trying to protect them. He provides us with guidance, instruction, and the Holy Spirit for our good. But we have to ask the following question and answer it honestly.

What are you buying into and what does it cost?

We buy into many abstracts every day – worth, success, lust, popularity, ambition, materialism – in efforts to keep up to speed with everyone else and (hopefully) find some sort of meaning for life. Chasing after these very things is what exhausts us and is reflective of the level of conformity we are struggling against. Has complacent conformity snuck into an area of your life? Do not abandon the process of transformation or passively allow the importance of spiritual renewal to get lost in the static. Check the price tag first.

Christine Parris

> "I am a girl who was born into a family with a generational curse of addiction."

Growing up with addicts as parents it seemed almost normal to get high. And so, I did. Until it eventually cost me everything. Family, kids, a home. Anything and everything – even my freedom.

Jail for me is where God put me to save me. I broke the chains of addiction through prayer, obedience, and the grace of God. Since then, he has restored all that I have lost and has blessed me with so much more than I could have ever thought possible.

PHILIPPIANS 1 6

JOHN 6 37

JOHN 6

JOHN 14 18

1 PETER 2 11

JEREMIAH 17 9

MATTHEW 6 33

JOSHUA 1 9

1 PETER 2 10

OVER
CO
ME

JEREMIAH 29 11

GALATIANS 5 1

PROVERBS 11 2

MATTHEW 11 28

EPHESIANS 2 10

1 PETER 5 8

PSALM 147 3

JOHN 16 33

MATTHEW 6 27

ROMANS 12 2

VIII

Regret and Discernment

THE AFTERMATH

We all make mistakes, some minuscule and some gargantuan. Yet, the tragedy is when we make mistakes that could have been avoided. Feelings such as regret, shame, and guilt customarily accompany this type of blunder. The wisest way to judge our decisions is by observing their outcomes. What did it create, destroy, or solve? Did it result in failure or success? As intellectual Christians, we can reverse engineer our motivations and work backward to gauge the validity of the decisions we make by evaluating the outcome.

Decisions, decisions, decisions. I'm sure we have all made decisions that we immediately grieved. Most of these choices, I would wager, have been made in the heat of a moment when emotions were high. Was the situation appraised logically or was it based on a feeling? Did we *know better*, as my grandmother used to say, but just didn't *do better*, even though we have seen the aftermath at least a dozen times or more?

The particularly tragic lesson from the do-better scenario resides in a moment, a split second after a hurtful word or an ill-conceived action occurs, when we awaken from the coma and realize the error of our way. It is almost like watching a train wreck develop in slow-motion, where all involved parties are stunned at what has just happened and are calculating how to respond. Abruptly, we are made conscious of the fact that our hands have created this faux pas and desperately search for CTRL+Z on the keyboard.

Every individual I have worked with in the past begins quantifying their length of recovery in days, then months, and finally in years. However, whether it was their first or hundredth attempt, a few of them measure their recovery in hours. Because it is usually right after a regretful decision, they are enlightened to what they have done and are becoming again. This habitual observation led to the subsequent statement:

Regret will always follow the decision to rebel.

DEDUCTIVE REASONING

The context of our scripture finds the apostle Paul writing to the church in Philippi when he was believed to be imprisoned in Rome for his spiritual beliefs. He could have chosen to conform and keep his head low, but he didn't. He chose to do what was right even though it would cost him his freedom and eventually his life. By human standards, his decision could be considered questionable. Thankfully for us, God is divine and at the steering wheel. Not a human scanning the radio dial, eating a biscuit, running late to work.

And I am sure of this, that he who began a good work in you will bring it to completion at the day of Jesus Christ.

Philippians 1:6

Before we go any further, I want to delineate the difference between guilt and shame using another one of my grandmother's sayings, "Are you sorry you did it, or sorry you got caught?" Whereas guilt is sorry for doing it, shame is sorry you got caught. Guilt is godly conviction, shame is not. Regret and remorse are products of disobedient decisions; an event occurring when we go against that inner conviction that guides and instructs us. Some call this beckoning expression a conscience. Others call it the Holy Spirit: the same voice that Jesus spoke of and promised.

And I will ask the Father, and he will give you another Helper, to be with you forever, even the Spirit of truth, whom the world cannot receive, because it neither sees him nor knows him. You know him, for he dwells with you and will be in you.

John 14:16-17

The more you listen to that little voice, the louder it gets. By contrast, the less you listen, the more silent it becomes. It is the practical concept of whatever you choose to feed is going to grow. But the good news is that we don't have to stay in this state of lament. Even when Adam and Eve were dealing with their regret, God had prepared a plan. We do things we will deplore because it is part of our sinful nature. As humans, we love the feeling of rebellion and getting away with something. Just as many relapses have occurred because of shame, as has pride been responsible for. Regret cultures the cycle of self-loathing, in which we continue to dull out and silence that little voice.

EMBRACE THE PROCESS

Some decisions are recoverable, and some are not. With the price tag being high for regrettable decisions (hurting others and ourselves), we are compelled to first reckon with what we are risking. To do this, we return to a section of our verse in Philippians – *He who began a good work in you*. There is a notion of progression found here, the process of God refining your character. It is the same sort of progressive discernment that is identified in the following verse:

When I was a child, I spoke like a child, I thought like a child, I reasoned like a child. When I became a man, I gave up childish ways.

1 Corinthians 13:11

Discernment is accepting and applying godly counsel and statutes for proper living. Learning to make decisions that you will not anguish and wail over is a profitable component of the 'good work' Paul speaks of. When you come to Christ, He begins a completely transformative process – a rather mysterious-sounding enterprise – that can be tangibly witnessed when we consciously weigh our actions and words. Warning though, this isn't the easiest endeavor to undertake if you cannot exhibit patience with the process of humility and be willing to resist knee-jerk reactions.

We will continue defining discernment the way the Hebrews and Greeks did, through the idea of thoughtful examination. Discernment is fighting the urge to react and asking what this choice will cost you or others. It is the idea of making decisions you won't regret because you were a puppet of your desires and emotions. While this may come off as esoteric, I assure you it is not. For this cause, we can establish a specific and concrete goal (in the form of a mission statement), that might say something catchy like:

The goal for today is to not do anything stupid that we will have to pay for tomorrow.

In all seriousness though, this endeavor requires commitment first and foremost. And a close second on that list is willing to let someone investigate your life from time to time. This should be someone you trust and someone you are ok being transparent with. They will act as your accountability. But all the burden is not just theirs to bear – it is a partnership – they have their responsibility and you have yours.

TWO OPTIONS

We will finish out this chapter with a contrast from two of Jesus' disciples. One of them made a horrific decision and chose not to process the consequences, while the other made an equally disturbing choice, but addressed it. One committed suicide, while the other received grace.

Then when Judas, his betrayer, saw that Jesus was condemned, he changed his mind and brought back the thirty pieces of silver to the chief priests and the elders, saying, "I have sinned by betraying innocent blood." They said, "What is that to us? See to it yourself." And throwing down the pieces of silver into the temple, he departed, and he went and hanged himself.

Matthew 27:3-5

Judas betrayed Jesus for silver. He listened to Satan and allowed a poor decision to lead to regret, which ultimately resulted in him committing suicide. Don't high-side on Judas just yet. To God, a sin is a sin, and all sin puts a distance between Him and us. There is no bell curve; betraying Jesus is the same as denying Him.

Peter on the other hand was adamant that he would never deny Jesus and even went as far as to say that he would die for Him. To which Jesus responded by telling him that he knew Peter would indeed deny Him… multiple times. After the rooster crowed and the words of Jesus came true, Peter experienced a tearful heartbreak, which led to repentance. This is the same Peter who would eventually be known as 'The Rock' that Jesus would build His church on. Both Peter and Judas were disloyal and unfaithful. The contrasting differences between the two outcomes were that Judas' betrayal was conspired and ended with no repentance, where Peter's denial was reactionary and led to a heart change.

And immediately the rooster crowed a second time. And Peter remembered how Jesus had said to him, "Before the rooster crows twice, you will deny me three times." And he broke down and wept.

Mark 14:72

Discernment is not just about knowing better; it is about acting accordingly and doing better – learning from your mistakes. Through repentance, God develops our character and carries on a good work. This progression is at the heart of recovery and is carried out through obedience and striving to do better, not staying in the same worn-out rut. Just because we have made bad decisions in the past, does not mean we are obligated to continue making them. This path of deduction finally leads us to the following summation:

If regret doesn't lead to repentance, it will only lead to remorse.

Ron Goss

> "When I was a kid, I lived in a neighborhood where all the houses were close together and in city blocks and there were several streets in the area that made up our neighborhood."

I loved playing outside all around the neighborhood from morning till dark. When it was time to come home my mom would go outside and stand on the front steps to our house and yell my name over and over again as loud as she could until she saw me walking up the street towards our house. If I didn't come home when she called, she would get in our car and drive around the neighborhood until she found me. Almost always that meant that I was going to get grounded for a couple of days for not being where I was supposed to be and coming home when called. Although it didn't always feel like it, her motives were always out of love for me, even when I was being corrected for not doing right.

2 Peter 3:9 Says "We are all God's children, God is patient with us, not wanting anyone to perish but everyone to come to repentance. I believe that God calls out to us very loudly to come to a relationship with him, to repent. Sometimes that voice is very soft, but we know it is Him calling. When we choose not to respond he does not just give up and go away, what kind of a loving Father would do that? Instead, he comes to find us just like it is described in the parable of the lost sheep in Luke 15:4 "Suppose one of you has a hundred sheep and he loses one of them. Doesn't he leave

the ninety-nine in the open country and go after the lost sheep until he finds it?" When God is calling us to come to him and we choose to ignore his voice, I believe he allows us to suffer the consequences of our own pride and desires until many of us hit what we call our "rock bottom". For most of us, it is only when we hit our rock bottom that we are still enough and desperate enough to surrender our will and our lives to Christ who is willing, waiting, and able to rescue us from our desperate selves.

I had been ignoring God's voice for quite some time when I hit my rock bottom in 2013 and my life crumbled into dust. Isaiah 26:5 says "He humbles the proud and brings down the arrogant city. He brings it down to dust." I found myself addicted to opiates and crack, my wife left me, and I was without a job and broke. Fortunately, my daughters loved me enough to intervene and insist that I get help. So, at 53 years old I entered a rehab for 45 days and that is when I realized how much God really loved me and how he felt about me. As I repented and asked God to forgive me Christ took my shame and regret and gave me the righteousness of Christ. God the Father now calls me His son!

From the day I walked out of that rehab God began to make me into a new man, the man he wants me to be. He is continually pruning and shaping me more into the image of Christ Jesus. God has blessed me beyond measure with a Godly wife who loves me, a job, a home, and a wonderful family of 7 children and 10 grandchildren. I have found that I am capable of the worst things that my mind can imagine. Any change and any goodness in me is not from my own self but it is from Christ Himself living in me. To God be the Glory for the things He has done!

OVERCOME

JOHN 6 37

PHILIPPIANS 1 6

JOHN 14 18

JEREMIAH 17 9

JOSHUA 1 9

1 PETER 2 11

MATTHEW 6 33

JEREMIAH 29 11

GALATIANS 5 1

PROVERBS 11 2

MATTHEW 11 28

EPHESIANS 2 10

1 PETER 5 8

PSALM 147 3

MATTHEW 6 27

JOHN 16 33

ROMANS 12 2

IX

Disappointment and Contentment

MISPLACED HOPE

More. More. More. Looking for things to fulfill us is a natural human instinct. Some would even say that we have been created to consume, and they would be correct. Accordingly, complications develop when we look to the patronage of this world to satisfy us when they are structurally incapable. We form unrealistic beliefs that crumble under the stress and lead to a feeling known as disappointment. Something has failed, yet again, to meet our hopeful expectations and destroyed our track record.

In the opening verse of Ecclesiastes, Solomon says "All is vanity." In effect, he uses the word *vanity* a total of thirty-seven times. His conscious decision to employ the oversaturation of this word is done for one purpose: that of impressing upon the reader that everything in this world is worthless and futile. Everything. He also uses the phrase 'striving after wind' to further elaborate on this maxim. Everything – wisdom, work, indulgence, wealth. He spends twelve chapters, 220 of the 222 verses, 5540 of the 5579 words contained within the book of Ecclesiastes (99.099099% by volume) all to develop a thesis – which is then delivered in the final two verses:

> The end of the matter; all has been heard. Fear God
> and keep his commandments, for this is the whole
> duty of man. For God will bring every deed into
> judgment, with every secret thing, whether good or
> evil.
>
> Ecclesiastes 12:13-14

FAULTY EXPECTATIONS

Most disappointments are conceived and reared during self-brooding episodes and obsessing over what we feel we deserve. For many of us, this is especially true when it comes time to acknowledge and celebrate our hard work and determination. If we have invested in something that doesn't turn out a certain way, we suddenly lose our sense of purpose. For others, it may be tied up in the misplaced importance of a particular identity or possession. We idolize these presumptions and expect them to make us feel whole and give our lives meaning, but the hunt becomes a pointless and impossible task. During this pursuit, we tragically tend to neglect the gifts God has given us because we are too preoccupied with sulking over misplaced awards.

When these expectations are not met, dissension, anger, depression, and self-medicating become the only trophies we have to show for our expeditions. Alternatively, and equally frustrating is when prospects only manage to temporarily subdue – never bringing with them a lasting feeling of joy or fulfillment. The burden of time confirms the weary realization that our idols have lost their shine and have once again let us down. We nurse our wounds, develop spiritual Alzheimer's, and spawn the cycle all over again once we see the next shiny trinket appear over the horizon.

When the suspicion of actually being an addict began to materialize, it was in the revelation and admission that something was absent. I needed something that just wasn't there. I thought it was another drink or a handful of pills. When in hindsight, it was a spiritual relationship with my Creator. I was content chasing for anything else to fill the void or at the very least, to numb it. I Goldilocks'd everything; not nearly enough of this, but way too much of that (moderation was never a strong characteristic I possessed). All reflective of the emotional rollercoaster that addiction takes you through.

In the John D. Rockefeller biography *Titan* written by Ron Chernow, Rockefeller disclosed his biggest concern regarding business by saying you should "Fear the peaks as much as you fear the troughs." The source of this wisdom seems coincidentally ironic though, given that John D. (born in 1839 and died in 1937) is still considered to be the wealthiest person in the history of the world, through acquiring and leveraging the sale of oil. (While it is considered purely speculative and accidental, the little guy with a top hat and monocle on the *Monopoly* board does bear a striking resemblance to him, in a weird doppelganger sort of way.) He was also the main reason the United States government passed the Sherman Antitrust act in 1890, to make sure corporations like his Standard Oil, would not grow that large and powerful again, forcing him to break the company up.

Interesting footnote, however, Rockefeller found a way around this antitrust dilemma and eventually used this law to aggressively increase his wealth in the long run. Nonetheless, another absurdly rich businessman, a Scottish steel magnate known by the name of Andrew Carnegie became involved in a practice known as philanthropy (donating large sums of money for public causes such as museums, universities, and of course Carnegie Hall) in which he and Rockefeller became viciously competitive at, in attempts to outdo the other to see who could give the most money away. Rockefeller, not allowing defeat, eclipsed the $350 million that Carnegie gave away by donating almost $150 million more. The reason I interject this biographical perspective is the fact that both these men, having reached the epitome of success, found that money and achievement did not secure contentment. While it certainly allowed them to serve others with amassed fortunes, the riches could not fill the vacuum left in the wake of acquiring their empires. I can't help but think there are two distinct parallels to this line of thought within our spiritual walks through recovery – the highs result in lows, and idols will fail to fulfill.

MULTITASKING

Our scripture reference comes from the Sermon on the Mount and occurs shortly after the Beatitudes. Ultimately it is a call to make sure you have your priorities correct in life. Jesus isn't saying "Do this and you'll get that house in the Bahamas and a Lambo." He is saying don't attempt to find fulfillment in the things of this world. Instead, make sure your spiritual relationship with God is at the top of that to-do list. Erroneously, we neglect seeking our spiritual development because we are distracted and divided when we seek *these things* to complete us.

But seek first the kingdom of God and his righteousness, and all these things will be added to you.

Matt 6:33

I estimate this verse to be both spiritual advice and an earthly warning. He is warning us to not find security in these things – people, professions, possessions. These things will leave you empty, defeated, and imbittered. The worldly search for fulfillment will only lead to disappointment, whether now or on your deathbed. Kids will break your heart, your spouse will take you for granted, jobs will be lost, health issues will come, and friends will migrate away. Material objects like cars will break down and fancy clothes will fade and go out of style. Everything at flea markets, yard sales, and thrift stores at one time was believed to possess the magical power of purpose and meaning but now find themselves in limbo of being thrown away or donated.

These things are valid concerns though. They are items we all need to survive – materials that we are provided with but may not quite be up to the standards we think we deserve. You start to look around and think "I want what that dude has" instead of recognizing what you have been given and expressing thankfulness and asking, "Am I being faithful with what God has entrusted me with already? How am I doing on the scale of being a faithful philanthropist?"

HUMBLE GRATITUDE

Disappointment serves no other function than to distract you with what you wished you had and forget about what you do have. You move from disappointment to contentment by being thankful and grateful; by being humble instead of a spoiled little brat. And the best way I have found to do this is by writing these things down as they come to mind, no matter how little or trivial you may think they are. After you initiate this intentional act of recognition, ask yourself, "How would God want me to use this 'thing' to build His kingdom?"

This suggested activity will assist in a growing appreciation for what you have been given, but more meaningfully, acknowledge who has given it to you and why. We humans tend to take gifts for granted, like waking up every morning, a sunrise in winter, a sunset in summer, a cold pillow, running water, a tangerine. It is all too casual to sweep this knowledge under the rug and continue the primal search that invariably decays us from the inside out; seeking out other stuff to put in the place of that which really matters.

A FINAL WORD

Much has been said regarding commitment on behalf of individuals seeking recovery from substance abuse and addiction. Many well-meaning and highly educated professionals state that an individual must *want* and seek recovery. Resultantly, when armed with this narrowed guidance, recovery – in and of itself – eventually becomes an idol and one of *these things*. While to some extent (albeit to a lesser degree), I agree and would confirm their guidance, despite it being foundationally flawed. True, if the individual is indeed committed to the cause, there is a better chance they may in fact obtain recovery if they see a value in it (as opposed to being forced into it when they are not really interested in entertaining the notion at all). Adversely though, that is not the long-term nemesis for addicts facing sustained recovery. The inherent flaw in this logic resides in a primary misunderstanding of the human relationship to oppositional challenges and the fluid progression of recovery. This oversight does not take seriously enough the proposition of *when* – not *if* – struggles come, how will the individual overcome them? To which I offer the inevitable alteration to their statement, as follows:

You *might* find recovery if that is what you are looking for. But seek Jesus and you *will* find much more.

Joseph M. Bohren

> "Well, my addiction started at the age of 8 years old."

I started using pot until I was 15 years old, then jumped to using meth and crack. I continually used that for over 25 years. In that 25 years, drugs took me through multiple jobs, two broken marriages, spending almost half of my life behind bars, the loss of kids, but most importantly the loss of myself.

I had no self-worth. I hated myself so bad that I tried suicide countless times. I cut my wrists, jumped in front of a moving car running about 35 mph, leaped off a thirty-foot cliff, and overdosed on pills. I just hated myself so much because of my addiction.

I have a 21-year-old son that I didn't talk to since he was 4 years old, from my first failed marriage. In my second marriage (which also ended in divorce), I have a daughter that is 14 now and was adopted. I have a set of twins with another lady, one boy and one girl. The boy died when he was 3 months old, but the girl is 6 now.

Addiction took everything from me. I was homeless and living in a tent for over 6 years, eating out of dumpsters and whatever I could get. I was a hopeless mess.

But I was sitting in my tent one day wanting to kill myself and I finally told the Lord if He wanted me to stop using drugs, then He would have to help me. So, 3 days later I got arrested and went to jail for drugs, again. I walked into the jail like I owned it. I waited to go to court to see what was going to happen. I was trying to get into rehab for the 15th time, but they intended for me to go to prison. So, I hit my knees and started praying for God to help me not to go to prison and let me go to rehab. This was the first time I've ever talked to a judge in my life. The judge let me go to rehab. I went to rehab for 90 days and completely sold out to the Lord.

When I came home from rehab, I came back to live on the streets for 3 or 4 nights. On the last day, somebody stole my stuff, and it was cold that night and rainy. I prayed to the Lord and told him if He lets me make it through the night, I would check in to the rescue mission. So, I did, and I stayed there for four months. Now, I have been living in a transitional house for the past two years and am also the house manager. I've got my driver's license back, a car, and my son that I have not talked to in 15 years.

I've met a lot of wonderful loving people. The Lord has used me to minister to the homeless by feeding, clothing, and showing them the way their life could be if they would just give it to the Lord. I've got all my kids in my life and do what the Lord wants. I love the Lord and He loves me. Thank you, Jesus, for this sober life.

X

Turmoil and Peace

PREPARE FOR CONFLICT

When obsessing over the circumstances of our situations, we can quickly become unstable in our environments and insecure of our identity. Most of the time this typhoon ramps up in our childhood and grows, and grows, and grows into an uncontrollable storm. Eventually, we start to mimic a tiny boat on a turbulent sea; tossed back and forth from wave to crashing wave. Our readiness for disaster and preparedness for an emergency can often be the difference between life and death during floods, earthquakes, and hurricanes. Shouldn't we also apply that same level of urgency when planning for probable spiritual storms?

Battle after battle, war after war, conflict is a non-stop certainty of life. However, the existence of confrontation is not restricted to the outside world only. On many occasions, these wars take place on the internal battleground: in our hearts and minds. Throughout the journey of teaching groups, I have come to the conclusion there are two main camps of individuals in recovery; those who are committed and those who are not. The lesson in this chapter is for the first group. It is a call for them to be aware of the costs that are involved. A level of measured appreciation for the expenditure and resulting conflict on the way is required for success. Jesus even referred to the need for this mindful calculation in the gospel of Luke.

For which of you, desiring to build a tower, does not first sit down and count the cost, whether he has enough to complete it?

Luke 14:28

In its entirety, Overcome was foundationally built around the verse of scripture we will anchor to in this chapter. The previous chapter ended with a short discussion on this concept of commitment, which we will continue to elaborate on more fully now, for a very specific reason. In the early days of recovery, it is naively easy to not take into account the importance of the fact that life is full of turmoil, and that turmoil has a tendency to steal your hope and reel you back into the tangled seas.

I assume I don't have to prod very much to get you to conjure up the sources of your greatest problems and difficulties in life. From recovery itself to making it through the day (and not flipping out on someone) to rebuilding a relationship, securing a job, finding a new place to live, and dealing with your family – the origins can cover the spectral gamut. Whatever it is, keep it in mind as we progress through this lesson. Because knowing what it is will help you better prepare for how to handle it.

PERSPECTIVE
Most of the turmoil we face in life is due to a lack of preparation for the probable. Preparation in this respect unfolds with the acknowledgment that we are a conflicted species. The chronicles of our existence are chaotic, to say the least. Our stories are narrated by how we have

historically behaved and responded to these conflicts, which in turn disclose our beliefs and character. Conflicts are trials and processes that either bring us closer to God or drive us further away from Him. One of the most fundamental means of having perspective in conflict is embodied in the following verse:

In this you rejoice, though now for a little while, if necessary, you have been grieved by various trials, so that the tested genuineness of your faith—more precious than gold that perishes though it is tested by fire—may be found to result in praise and glory and honor at the revelation of Jesus Christ.

1 Peter 1:6-7

Yes, you read that correctly; rejoice in the trials. In the second edition of *The Resistance*, we explore this suggestion in greater detail, but essentially, our faith and character are required to undergo these trials and tests. Due to free will, we must choose to submit to undergoing these periods of refinement and let the impurities bubble up to the surface to then be dealt with. Trials will come, but the extent of our suffering and relative outcomes will be determined by how we embrace this process. Categorically, these sources of trials come in three flavors: internal, external, and eternal.

INTERNAL

As Christ-followers, most of our conflict resides internally. We are pulled in opposite directions between what is right and what is wrong – between desires and wisdom. If you are a disciple, Christ-follower, Christian, you will almost always have internal conflict. This is where the self is its own worst enemy. The self chooses to rebel against proper wisdom and instruction because of its desires. We find this conflict presented as plainly as possible in the book of Romans.

For I do not understand my own actions. For I do not do what I want, but I do the very thing I hate… For I know that nothing good dwells in me, that is, in my flesh. For I have the desire to do what is right, but not the ability to carry it out.

Romans 7:15, 18

Paul is not lackadaisically being difficult or convoluted. We exhibit a combative duality. We are flesh and spirit. Temporal and eternal. Water carried in a vessel. Smoke within a jar. This struggle is not just limited to recovering addicts, it is common to all people. Our goal while on this Earth is for the spirit to hopefully subdue the flesh, not the other way around. The body will eventually return to the dust and the spirit will return to the One who gave it, to determine its eternal destination. The key to handling internal conflict though is to think *eternally*. Which we will get to in a moment after we cover the second source.

EXTERNAL
External or relational conflict usually finds itself to be the most publicly displayed and entertaining. It is the most recognized because it theatrically puts the onus and spotlight on a potentially wide array of suspects, rather than us and our actions. (Due to the inability – or perhaps stubbornness – to get along or see eye to eye with specific people. Because of this, a large portion of external conflict is occasionally misunderstood to be habitual and serial, when in reality it was nothing more than a case of 'wrong day and wrong time.') Many of the struggles we face coming via this avenue

are due to our mishandling of reactions and (in all honesty) poor communication skills. Spiritual maturity allows us to shift our perception and recognize these confrontations as opportunities for further targeted growth.

The following scripture from James puts this notion of reframing emphasis into somewhat of a logical series of events. Tragically, it is usually only after we have gone through the conflict and begin to bandage our wounds, do we see the full scope of it, firsthand.

Count it all joy, my brothers, when you meet trials of various kinds, for you know that the testing of your faith produces steadfastness. And let steadfastness have its full effect, that you may be perfect and complete, lacking in nothing.

James 1:2-4

ETERNAL

Now that we have covered the easier sources of conflict to identify, we must acknowledge the last source – one that we take for granted regularly because we do not see it with the naked eye – the eternal conflict and the resulting value we associate with it. In other words, the struggle to accept the idea of an afterlife. What makes this such a difficult fight is simply the labor involved in restraining fleshly desires is rather exhausting at times.

If we indeed believe there is a heaven and that we are not of this world, then technically that belief should directly impact how we live this physical life here on this terrestrial plane. Spiritually, there are forces at play that we don't see, who come bearing guerilla-style strategies and tactics. Much to our chagrin, we mistakenly overlook this source of conflict and routinely regard the afterlife as something fantastically mythological. Because after all, our enemy knows the easiest way to defeat an opponent is to get them to not even show up to the field. This is not done by convincing them they will lose the fight, but rather by suggesting the fight does not exist in the first place.

For we do not wrestle against flesh and blood, but against the rulers, against the authorities, against the cosmic powers over this present darkness, against the spiritual forces of evil in the heavenly places.

Ephesians 6:12

(A quick disclaimer about spiritual forces before we continue any further. While I do believe there are angels and demons at work, but to what degree, I do not know. How they work or even why they do what they do, I cannot fully decipher neither. Chances are the next statement may offend or even be a little controversial, but I am ok with it as long as it encourages people to seek God and pray to understand the issue better. Nevertheless, there appears to be an alarming trend where a person will make a selfish, sinful decision then chalk it up to demonic intervention – "We're under attack!" In doing this, they are crafting an escape plan and scapegoat when they do not take responsibility for their choices. How can we expect God to convict and then forgive us for these decisions if we are always trying to shift the blame to Satan?)

THE GRAVITY OF THE SITUATION
The account of the last supper begins in John chapter 13 and goes through chapter 17. While the Synoptic Gospels (Matthew, Mark, and Luke) all give reports of the last supper, only John gives this level of behind-the-scenes

detail. These five chapters in John encapsulate an intimate setting and provide a portrait of Jesus spending His last hours with the disciples – men that He led, taught, and spent the past three years of His life with. He intended to reaffirm and prepare them for the difficulties that awaited them. During this account, He washes their feet, calls out Judas for future betrayal, promises the Holy Spirit, encourages them to endure the coming persecution, foretells His own death and resurrection, commands them to love one another just as He has loved them, and tells them about the preparation of a place for them in heaven. In chapter 14 verse 1, He tells them to "not let their hearts be troubled." Thereby addressing all three categories of conflict in one single statement. This troubling in our hearts is where conflict is born, springs forth from, and returns back to.

I have said these things to you, that in me you may have peace. In the world you will have tribulation. But take heart; I have overcome the world.

John 16:33

For our anchor verse above, imagine the inner conflict going on in this scene: Jesus knows that Judas is going to betray Him, and everyone will scatter and deny him. He knows He is going to be subjected to a humiliating and painful death. He knows the plan of God rests on His obedience – even unto death – for the sakes of the very ones whose sin has and will continue to place Him on the cross. As far as literature goes, this is the climax of the story. Sixty-six books of canonized and inspired writing spanning thousands of years and numerous authors. 31,102 verses (3,779 in the gospels alone) all pointing towards or emanating outward from His upcoming work on the cross.

Not waxing poetic, but this is the epicenter of a soul-quake and the culmination of everything that has preceded and ever will proceed from in our human history. Jesus acknowledged the gravity of the situation and did not run from it or ignore it. He understood what was at stake, not only for the disciples but for all who would follow. We witness the effects of this struggle on Him (after the last supper has finished) while He is praying in the garden of Gethsemane. We see Him sweating blood during repeated prayers to "take this cup". But He shows His obedience to the Father by confirming "but Your will be done." He knew the gravity of the situation and confronted it, head-on.

NO QUARTER

Whatever conflict you are facing right now, you have but three options: ignore it, run from it and try to hide, or run to God and His word. Ignoring problems only buys you a few more moments of blissful ignorance at best. Attempting to outrun conflict will only result in exhaustion and having to engage in wearied combat when finally apprehended. The only logical conclusion is to seek God. Our aim is to be well prepared when the waves start crashing in; not running to the local hardware store for plywood and sandbags in the middle of a torrential downpour (and yes, they are obviously sold out, because everyone else is panic buying). The best way we can prepare is to acknowledge the turmoil and seek His word on it. Acting like the dissonance isn't there or that it will not happen to you is short-sighted and careless.

For us to stay committed to our spiritual walks and recovery, we must accept the possibility and probability that specific moments exist that will test the resolve of our character and our faithful commitment to Jesus. Chances are everything is not going to be roses and rainbows from day one. Family members may not welcome you back with open arms. Friends may never trust you again. Finding a job may be near impossible. Which is precisely why He ends this verse with "But take heart, I have overcome the world." We do not rely on our own strength or temporary victories; we hold fast to His ultimate victory. Even when it seems like we are taking a relentless volley of artillery from the enemy and are about to lose yet another battle, He has already won the war. Hold fast, these assaults are the final gasps of a dying opponent and a last-ditch effort to destroy as much as they can. As long as you abide with Jesus, you will prevail.

Many have asked what I held on to during the early stages of recovery. I perceive this inquiry to align with the nautical phrase *the bitter end*. The bitter end is a link in the chain of an anchor. More specifically, it is the last link of the chain that connects the anchor to the boat. The anchor is heavy and has these hook-shaped protrusions, called flukes, which dig into the seafloor. Additionally, in popular terms, the bitter end means the conclusion of a troublesome and unpleasant situation. Both of these descriptions are reflective of my recovery.

During the time I found my rock bottom I had no support system and was outcasted and alienated due to my actions. All the chain had run out of the locker, but the flukes never found anything to dig into. Through the course of the honeymoon stage of recovery, situations will subtly present themselves and serve as warning signs. Pay attention to these signals – they will arrive in the form of specific places, certain people, movies, music – things that beckon the old self to awaken again. The pivotal step in preparing for this stage is knowing where those traps lie and what your anchor is. For me, the bitter end was found in one verse of scripture.

> but God shows his love for us in that while we were
> still sinners, Christ died for us.

Romans 5:8

This single verse put my entire life into context. I was an enemy toward God, but He still loved me. I felt like the least deserving person to have ever walked the face of the Earth. The chain not only ran out, but it was in the process of exceeding its tensile strength and disintegrating. There was nothing I did that warranted any reason for me to continue living. Figuratively, all I accomplished with the totality of my life up to that point was aiming my ship toward the jagged and jutting rocks along the coastline, intent on hitting them at full speed.

In all honesty, I believe Jesus reached out and took hold of the remaining chain to keep me from certain physical death, but more tremendously to prevent my soul from perishing as well, just to give me one more moment to make a choice. And He did all of this, while I was still His enemy. He died to save me, and it broke my heart. How can you hate or even run away from a love like that – a love that is willing to die for you, just to give you one more opportunity to experience a life of peace and rest for your troubled soul?

Find your anchor before it is too late.

Chastity Bloomfield

> "I was in the 9th grade when I first started experimenting with alcohol and drugs."

The wrong kinds of friends, the wrong places, and the wrong choices led me to use Xanax. The pills made me feel better. They made me feel like I fit in. I spiraled farther into my addiction and completely out of control when my parents divorced when I was 16 years old. I wondered if it was my fault. I was confused and angry and hurt.

I turned to drugs and alcohol for comfort and for an escape from the pain I felt. By the age of 23, my addiction had consumed me in every way, and I experienced another major loss through a breakup with a boyfriend I had been in a relationship with for ten years. My physical health was very poor, I weighed only 98 pounds. My mental and emotional health had also deteriorated, and I was so depressed I couldn't see any hope for my life.

I was not raised in the church, but by this time both of my parents were attending church and they were praying for me. They could see how bad my addiction had gotten and they confronted me. I was admitted to the hospital for detox and my life began to change.

Shortly after that, I attended a revival service with my dad and that is where I surrendered my life to God and was saved! I didn't change overnight, it took time, but God gave me the strength to completely stop taking Xanax and took the craving for alcohol away from me. I am still a work in progress, but I have devoted my life to God and now I help other people who are lost in addiction find hope in Christ!

OVERCOME

JOHN 6 37

PHILIPPIANS 1 6

JOHN 14 18

JEREMIAH 17 9

JOSHUA 1 9

1 PETER 2 11

MATTHEW 6 33

JEREMIAH 29 11

GALATIANS 5 1

PROVERBS 11 2

MATTHEW 11 28

EPHESIANS 2 10

1 PETER 5 8

PSALM 147 3

MATTHEW 6 27

JOHN 16 33

ROMANS 12 2

XI

Deception and Integrity

TO THE BITTER END

There once was a quote about weaving a tangled web I am sure we have all heard from our grandparents before. Deception is an extortionate game and I'm not sure of many instances it has ever paid off in the long run. When we attempt to deceive others, only one party is privy to the charade. But, when we resolve to deceive ourselves, we make a concerted effort to justify the lie by replacing reality with our own invented beliefs. Playing pretend was fun, as a child. At some point though, we have to put away the nunchucks and realize we aren't space ninja cowboys anymore.

Throughout this book, we have been dissecting motivating factors for addiction. In this chapter, we will be primarily looking at a casualty of not only addiction but of sin in general: our character. Previously, we discussed preparing for conflict by remaining committed. An expressed component of that commitment is actively engaging in the rebuilding of our reputation and character.

This chapter could easily be spread out over a couple of hundred pages, but for the sake of expedience, we will provide a few postcards from highlights on the map if you will. So, we will not be covering deception in great detail. I'm sure we all know what it is and why we humans do it. Instead, we will be exploring a single word and an idea, *completeness.* Because in all honesty, having a lesson that only focuses on deception instead of elaborating on integrity is like having a lawnmower in the desert... not very useful.

So, why don't we rip the band-aid off and get this ugly bit of work out of the way so we can move forward? While it is patently hypocritical to beat another person up over stupid decisions (no one wants to be 'should-ed' on all the time), I'm pretty sure most people have a conscience and already know what a bad choice smells like when they step in it. We are also painfully aware of how crafty our species is at duping, hoodwinking, bamboozling, snookering, flimflamming, two-faced double-dealing tomfoolery, swizzling, fibbing, and hornswoggling. Yes, we have taken to inventing words and phrases that take some of the sting out, but they all mean the same thing: lying.

PRIMING THE CANVAS

In any event, deception is the absence of truth, and it originates from the heart. It will always be motivated by some selfish gain (if you drill down deep enough). We often lie to get what we want or make excuses for why we didn't do what we knew we should have. Occasionally, others are not the only recipient of lies. A prominent and even more detrimental falsehood for those in recovery is believing they will never be sober or clean.

The truth is you can recover and live a life of recovered integrity. However, on the flip side, once you start feeding the stray cat of deception, it will show back up at your door begging. Then before you know it, it is in heat and has attracted all the neighborhood tomcats to your house. Suddenly, you are surrounded by meowing felines, and no one wants to come to visit anymore. The euphemism here is: lies are like cats, chase them off before you get surrounded by litter boxes and known as the crazy cat lady.

> And let steadfastness have its full effect, that you may
> be perfect and complete, lacking in nothing.

James 1:4

Underline the word *complete*. For a moment, I want you to mentally picture the underbelly of a ship, the hull of a vessel. When it is free from defects or voids, the integrity of the hull is considered intact. If that hull has been damaged, it is said to be compromised (fractures in the hull that go unnoticed during inspections are often the major contributing factor for the capsizing of boats, large or small). The way we describe integrity is with words like honest, moral, whole, undivided, trustworthy, peaceful, blameless. We do what we say we are going to, and we act the same in every situation.

Integrity describes the quality of our character. Integrity seeks completeness through obedience and truth. Where deceptions such as omission (intentionally withholding information) and commission (deliberately communicating that which is false, also known as *perjury* in a court of law) exist, obtaining completeness will be an impossibility. (As lawyers can attest, as I am sure most parents will affirm, how a question is constructed will many times determine if the plaintiff – or toddler – is going to be guilty of omission or commission. Asking a child if they are *done* cleaning their room may yield a possibly much different answer than asking if they have *completely* cleaned their room.)

WHO DO YOU THINK YOU ARE
To gain integrity, rebuilding our character obviously becomes an important priority of our recovery, whether it is recognized or not. In order to do this, we must predominantly see a value for the effort. The following questions are meant to spur you on to consider the worth of

such an undertaking. Understand, I inventory these quite frequently to make sure what I am saying and doing truthfully lines up with who I think I am. We may have discrepancies here and there, but over time, what will your decisions say about you? Just don't answer them quite yet...

>> If someone close to you were asked to use three words to describe you, what would they be?
>> What will your eulogy sound like? Would it sound any different depending on who was chosen to deliver it?

Granted, the previous inquiries are rather harsh. But choose to take accurate harshness over vague gentleness, any day of the week when given the option. However, developing integrity doesn't just occur overnight – we a spiritual work in progress.

For we are his workmanship, created in Christ Jesus
for good works, which God prepared beforehand,
that we should walk in them.

Ephesians 2:10

To fully appreciate this verse, take a few minutes to read Ephesians 2:1-10. This passage of scripture is amazingly rich with context – dead in our trespasses, carrying out the desires of the body and the mind, by grace you have been saved – one could easily write tomes of literature just from these ten verses. But for right now, absorb these scriptures and allow them to echo in your mind before answering the previous questions. Answering them was a sobering realization that I had indeed lost my way and didn't have the slightest bit of direction in life. It was a venture I didn't want to take but knew I would have to. But in order to set off on this journey (and not wind up talking to a volleyball on a remote and deserted island), it is respectable to set a true north and calibrate our compass with three facts. Fact number one: we are implored to acknowledge who God is. Reasonably it makes logical sense to start with the beginning verse of the Bible:

In the beginning, God created the heavens and the earth.

Genesis 1:1

If you can concede that God is responsible for all creation, then the foundation of the work is done. But truthfully, we don't typically get hung up on the generalities, as much as the specificities. Second, we must then accept who Jesus is:

Jesus said to him, "I am the way, and the truth, and the life. No one comes to the Father except through me.

John 14:6

Our compass needle normally exhibits reluctance with accepting that Jesus is the only way. We try to force north by attempting to work our way to salvation, like holding a magnet to the compass. This predisposition to bypass or subvert the process leads us to a final effort: realize and be cautiously aware of who we are:

The heart is deceitful above all things, and desperately sick; who can understand it?

Jeremiah 17:9

SEEK COMPLETENESS

The road to rebuilding our character is fraught with obstacles and opportunities. It is in these moments that we find chances to not only develop integrity but to show others what God has done for us. Many of you may forever be on trial with cynical family members that doubt your truthfulness. Like an onion, if you peel back enough layers, the present suspicions are usually warranted because they wreak of past offenses.

A final consideration for picturing integrity can be found down the same avenue as the hull of a ship, but with a husk. Envision the furry coat of a coconut or the leaved layers on an ear of corn. Once this protective covering is damaged, what happens? Everything inside becomes exposed and ruined. Untruthfulness will deteriorate our integrity in the same fashion as a blight upon a cornfield. This is why farmers preventatively spray pesticides on their crops, to keep the bugs away. Bugs, just like sin, hunt for and exploit the tiniest of cracks. And sin, just like bugs, can reproduce at an aggressive rate.

Lying is a sin that duplicates – just like feral cats, although you don't necessarily know how the little mutant offspring will turn out. For a final example, long ago you could make dozens of duplicates of something on a Xerox machine, which was great. Place the original on the scanner bed, type in a number, and hit start. A few days pass and you come to find out you have drastically underestimated how many copies you needed by a few hundred. You don't have the original anymore, but a copy of the original. Any defects, such as being slightly off-center, a crease, or smear of peanut butter on the bottom corner, will now show up on every copy that is made from that one, except slightly more noticeable. Lies and the complexities of deception magnify every time one is told. It is no longer just a little lie; it has now grown into an elaborate cover-up scheme, and every time it hits a new level of replication, it mutates and expands.

Since we can't go back in time and prevent our duplicities from occurring, we must seek to make amends the best we can and let present and future actions speak where our words have fallen short in the past. Rhythmically, we often find ourselves doing well for a short time, only to run into a moment of vulnerability. If we revert to old habits when faced with this test, we start to slide backward like a vehicle on a perilously ice-covered hill. That is why this sub-section is titled *seek* completeness, not *obtain* completeness. Completeness will never be obtained on this side of heaven, but we are expected to keep moving forward. God gives us opportunities to walk in good works and move forward instead of falling and sliding down the hill. Bad decisions in the past do not require bad decisions in the future. It may appear to be easier and cheaper to deceive at that moment but comes at a greater price in the end.

To end the breeding of lies (like Bob Barker always instructed us to do at the end of The Price is Right – by spaying and neutering the vagrant mongrel *Felis catus*) we must confess and repent. There is literally no other way to gain integrity. We all struggle with being obedient to God and often find ourselves allowing other things to take His position in our hearts. Confess the deception so conviction can take place. Repent from where you have fallen and get back up. We do this because we believe in what Jesus did for us. If He was willing to die to pay for our sins, do you believe He is going to lead you astray about how you should live the life He has called you to?

Beth Blackwell

> "I've always heard that saying – sin will take you farther than you ever meant to go, keep you longer than you wanted to stay, and cost you more than you intended to pay – but I didn't think that applied to me."

I really believed I could get high just sometimes, that no one would ever know and that I wasn't hurting anyone else. I had convinced myself I was in control. I was wrong. It didn't take long for my addiction to consume every part of my life and take everything from me. I lost my marriage, my children, my home, my career, my car. But it didn't stop there.

My addiction also took my dignity, my self-respect, my self-esteem, and then one night my addiction almost took my life when I overdosed. All the things I said I'd never do, I did. All the places I said I'd never go, I went. After years spent in the insanity of addiction, I was homeless and hopeless. I went to rehab as a last resort, and it was there that I met God and my life was changed.

That change didn't happen overnight. I still have to fight for my sobriety daily and I am still paying the consequences of my choices, but I found freedom from the chains of addiction. I took back control of my life from my addiction and relinquished that control to God and slowly but surely, He is restoring me back to everything I lost and destroyed in my addiction.

OVER
CO
ME

PHILIPPIANS 1 6
JOHN 14 18
JEREMIAH 17 9
JOSHUA 1 9
JOHN 6 37
JEREMIAH 29 11
GALATIANS 5 1
PROVERBS 11 2
MATTHEW 11 28
1 PETER 2 11
MATTHEW 6 33
EPHESIANS 2 10
1 PETER 5 8
PSALM 147 3
JOHN 16 33
ROMANS 12 2
MATTHEW 6 27

XII

Captivity and Freedom

WHOA, HOLD UP

The word captivity conjures up suspicions that some 'one' or some 'thing' has control over you. It could be the inhumane act of slavery itself, the result of a lost battle and you are now hostage, or complete absorption in thoughts or activities. The majority of time, whatever it is that holds you captive could care less about your safety and well-being. You wait for a commercial break, skip meals, forfeit sleep, and jump when it says jump. Shackled and in chains, you do what it says to do when it says to do it.

Throughout this chapter, we will be using some Old Testament, churchy sounding terms like *sin*, *sacrifice*, *confession*, *repentance*, and *glory*. I will attempt to describe them in a way to illustrate their essence and hopefully clear up some of the mysticism that may be surrounding them. A comprehensive grasp of these words is critical for taking hold of the contrast between being a slave to sin or walking in the freedom of Christ. I honestly believe that if we can get this truism down, it holds the key to unlock a potential turning point in our lives, both presently and for eternity.

In past attempts to persuade, I have humbly accepted the realization that I will never be a salesman. There is nothing I can say or do that will affect what someone will buy into and believe unless I act haywire. Then they might fancy me to be all sixes and sevens. Thankfully for both of us, trying to change what another person believes is not my job. My function is to illustrate as clearly as I can, what I believe and reflect that in my outer words and actions. Although failure (instead of success) seems to be the more consistent outcome despite best attempts, we carry on.

At some point in each of our walks, beliefs originated as a full-on struggle and then migrate to either being accepted as fact or discarded as fiction. If a belief is wrong and the appraisal stage is skipped, our 'foundation' soon starts to shift to accommodate this temporary annoyance – the squeaky wheel now controls the steering wheel, simply by tweaking the driver. While there are varying degrees of beliefs, we either shore them up with facts to brace their structural integrity, or we allow them to erode because we never devoted the required attention to inspecting them. Ignoring or acting like the presence of the three following facts are not true does not make them any less factual, the same way that gravity does not require our belief to exist.

1. We all sin. Humans will always err to the side of humanity. Our species is notorious for sinful behavior. Sin essentially means the active (not passive) choice to go against what God has said. Sin is rooted within the *self* and does not evaluate the cost or the outcome. Simply put, it means chasing your desires regardless of the damage it creates.

2. Sin will always lead to suffering. That suffering may take the form of spiritual, physical, mental, or emotional slavery and separation from a Holy God, family members, and friends. Sin hurts, sin is deadly and the debt it creates has to be paid somehow. Just like in the garden of Eden when Adam and Eve first sinned. God *sacrificed* an animal to cover their rebellion. The animal lost its life and they lost Eden.

3. We, ourselves, cannot remedy sin and suffering in any lasting way. The best we can hope for is to embrace a distraction and adopt the deception. Therefore, we cannot achieve success when attempting to earn our freedom. When we engage in this activity, we are attempting to justify ourselves by balancing the scales in a court of law. Without realizing the fact that the law is meant to condemn the accused, not provide a path to freedom.

These three facts are the basis for assessing the severity of our situation; as Romans 3 says "all have sinned and fall short of the Glory of God." Once we attain this level of awareness and maturity, these facts will compel us toward the following two actions:

1. Confession of one's sins is when we accept responsibility for our thoughts and actions. We stop hiding in the sin and admit that the criminal is the one in the mirror looking back at us. This isn't done to beat ourselves up through self-hate, but instead to be truthful and humble; we aren't gods. We then go to God and confess our misdeeds so we can ask Him for forgiveness. We do this because He is just and merciful. As scripture says, "He is faithful to forgive."

2. Repentance is a Greek military term that means to turn around. Imagine a squadron marching due east when the drill sergeant bellows "Halt." The procession comes to an abrupt stop. The sergeant then yells out "About face. Forward march." and the entire squadron spins on their heels and immediately marches west. In our spiritual lives, repentance means that we will stop going in the direction that is rebellious to God's command and walk in the

completely opposite direction. This process of repentance does not require a doctorate in theology or a master's of divinity to embark upon. It doesn't need some fancy worded, elegant prayer or a well-lit musical production. It does however demand honesty, humility, and faith.

IF YOU ARE FREE...

Which would you say were responsible for influencing you the most: a) *thoughts*, b) *beliefs*, or c) *actions*? I am convinced one of these is the primary, dominant driving force for each of us. If something gains control over you, it stands to reason that it will dictate how you handle situations, treat others, and even what you would choose to kill or die for.

Suppose I now ask what freedom means to you, could you answer the question confidently? As a teenager, what did it feel like when you got a little taste of freedom from your parents and their rules, if even for an hour? We sowed our wild oats and learned about the real-world – stuff you can't learn about while sheltered under your parent's roof. For example, our first speeding ticket. Hopefully, we then learned not to speed again. Hopefully...

For freedom Christ has set us free; stand firm therefore, and do not submit again to the yoke of slavery.

Galatians 5:1

In Galatians 5:1, notice Paul says at the end of the verse "...and do not submit again..." *Again*. For commonplace reasons, we enjoyed the thrill of breaking the rules while in our teens and young adult years. We would go back to school and re-live the entire moment over to our friends, again and again. But, as cause and effect soon reveal, a cost is associated with earning this bragging right (reference our previous discussion regarding yokes in chapter four). Our insurance premium has now skyrocketed, which means we will now have to figure out how to cover the cost. Some of our freedom, in the form of time, is about to be reallocated in the form of getting a part-time job or working additional hours to cover the extra expense. There is a corresponding cost with every exchange.

While a speeding ticket is a fairly harmless example, within it exists a core element – one illustrated by Eleanor Roosevelt's famous quote "With freedom comes responsibility." Thankfully, Jesus secured this freedom for us ahead of time. Our responsibility is to resist submitting *again*. If the desires of your heart are constantly leaving you to pick up the check, if your primal habits are dictating your very existence day-to-day, or if the relentless belief that God is disconnected and distant, we need to wipe the sleep from our eyes and realize we are bound in slavery to something other than God's truth and design.

...WHAT ARE YOU DOING WITH YOUR FREEDOM

At any given moment during the day, I am submitting to something; the only variable is what is being served. Am I indulgently submitting to myself, desires, pursuits of fame and fortune? Or am I serving a loving God that has supplied me with talents and gifts to build His kingdom – something that is everlasting and non-temporal? What you are held captive by reveals itself through polarities of what the heart values. Earthly pursuits appear to be the most pressing and serious to the heart but are trivial and decaying. While heavenly efforts may come off as somewhat nonchalant and detached, they are gravely the most urgent and multiplying.

Deteriorate or magnify? As Jesus pointed out, the Earth decays, and the gospel parlays.

"Do not lay up for yourselves treasures on earth, where moth and rust destroy and where thieves break in and steal, but lay up for yourselves treasures in heaven, where neither moth nor rust destroys and where thieves do not break in and steal. For where your treasure is, there your heart will be also.

Matthew 6:19-21

While we may not declare it verbally, we certainly act like the Christian walk is an activity devoid of freedom and joy. We let notions (temptations) of missing out on something 'fun' irritate our spiritual wisdom long enough until we have been coaxed into subjugation (sin). The same principle of how fishing lures entice with flash while concealing a barbed hook. (At least how they work for some people. For those like myself, fishing lures are an easy way to add decorative ornaments to overhanging trees at the lake.)

Concluding this chapter, we will consider the *what* and the *why* (two of the Five W's) of our beliefs, thoughts, and actions. When we are in slavery, we are unable to fully love God with all of our heart, soul, and might. We are divided and spiritually incapable of experiencing what true freedom feels like, looks like, and tastes like. Choosing to be a slave to sin prevents the ability to walk in freedom. We may want to be free, but our actions say otherwise. Consistent choices dictate what we really believe. Words and even actions may lie, but outcomes never do. The excuse of coincidence is what keeps souls in slavery. You cannot accidentally and consistently secure the same outcome over and over again without having worked towards it; no one is *that* lucky.

So, is all hope lost? Not even close. The Bible gives clear instruction for *what* (our first W) we must do to escape captivity – and we don't even have to learn Hebrew or go on a long journey to interpret the implied meaning:

You shall love the Lord your God with all your heart and with all your soul and with all your might.

Deuteronomy 6:5

Love the Lord. Love with everything you have. In loving the Lord, you will conversely hate sin, the very thing that seduces you into captivity. This love is a devotional attachment, similar to the bond of marriage, but stronger and deeper than any physical relationship you will ever know on Earth. Relationships on Earth take place between two screwed-up people, so the sum of that relationship will be flawed due to competing inconsistencies – parents to offspring, spouse to spouse, friend to friend. Both parties will eventually fail the other one, multiple times.

Whereas instead of the relationship with the Lord being a composition between two parties with defects, only one has blemishes and shortcomings. The other one is perfect. Since He is perfect (and still chooses to love us), we are able to at least experience what a constant, perfect love is supposed to be. Only then do we have the opportunity to experience what true freedom is. We can love Him completely, through His example. As scripture says, "We love because He first loved us."

The next verse is where we find our freedom – in the *why*. If you are a single mother, a factory worker, a recovering alcoholic, a school bus driver, a mechanic, a struggling artist, a landscaper, a teacher, a father, a daughter; do it with the determination of bringing *glory* to God. This is the why you do what you do. It took a while for me to appreciate this, at least on a keener level. For someone who is tied up in action and works, what we are doing always seems to be the most crucial piece of the puzzle, but it is not. Why you are doing something reveals the motivation and heart behind it.

And whatever you do, in word or deed, do everything in the name of the Lord Jesus, giving thanks to God the Father through him.

Colossians 3:17

In whatever it is you are doing, do it in the name of Jesus. Do it for the sacrifice He made for you – in honor and appreciation. Being mindful of why you are doing something will also help alleviate some of the burden of choosing to engage in destructive and sinful behavior. Being hateful, in the name of Jesus is ridiculous theology. Just as mindless as getting high to bring glory to the name of God. Pause to question why you have this certain belief, or why you think this specific way, or even why are you occupied with this decided action.

So, if you are free – what are you doing with your freedom? Are you returning to patterns that encourage a lifestyle of slavery to sin or are you walking out your freedom through a relationship with Jesus Christ? Can you say that whatever it is you are doing – is being done in the name of Jesus for God's glory?

David Marsh

"My relationship started out in the most glamorous way."

A homeless drug addict living out of the back of his car who heard that God loved him and proved it by sending His Son to die on the cross for my sin. That night I cried out for salvation and grace and found that the next day I woke up: changed. I wanted God and I didn't want drugs any longer. I sought after him hard and saw Him work in my life. Let's be honest; I lost my friends, my job, and my social life. What I gained was a relationship with God that began to consume me. My heart had turned toward him, and my life turned around.

I met my wife shortly after that and became involved in my local church. I felt God's call on my life presently after salvation and jumped into that calling. Then it happened… When God saved me that day, He changed my heart, but my mind was still very persuaded by the habits and triggers I had created over years of addiction and I fell. I was devastated, destroyed, and confused. How could I have done that to Jesus? I couldn't tell anyone. What would they think? I had to stay quiet and get back to where I had fallen. But I couldn't, so I let it progress in my isolation and darkness. I fell hard and fast. Once I opened that door in my life, it seemed almost impossible to shut. It ruined relationships that God had restored and brought me to places I swore to never go again. Then it happened confession, repentance and restoration flooded my life, and the hope that God wasn't finished yet.

I wish I could say that this was a one-time occurrence, but it wasn't. I fell into a cycle. A cycle of highs with God and lows with drugs. I tried almost everything I could think of to stop the cycle, but it never lasted. There are no physical solutions to spiritual problems. I was broken and eventually just gave up and succumb to the pangs of addiction. But God… I had finally reached my low and cried out to God in desperation. I loved Him. I wanted to serve Him, but I always stood in the way. Through a series of events, I confessed again. My marriage was hurting, my job was hurting and most importantly, my relationship with God was hurting. I ended up stopping everything in my life in a moment. I gave up my company, gave back my car, and we moved in with my in-laws. I went away to rehab.

At rehab, I fully surrendered my life to God and watched Him restore His calling for me to be a minister of the Gospel of Christ. After rehab, I remember one night I was at the beach and I went for a walk alone around midnight. I had to walk past a bar to get to the beach and when I finally got there I was struggling with temptation. I asked God how I am supposed to stay sober for the rest of my life? I'll never forget His answer. "I don't need you to stay sober forever, just for tonight; go back." I strive to live my life that way now in constant communion and relationship with Christ one decision at a time. When I got saved God changed my heart, but He has been constantly working to renew my mind each and every day through His Word and the decisions that I make.

PHILIPPIANS 16

JOHN 6 37

JOHN 14 18

JEREMIAH 17 9

1 PETER 2 11

MATTHEW 6 33

JOSHUA 1 9

OVERCOME

JEREMIAH 29 11

GALATIANS 5 1

PROVERBS 11 2

MATTHEW 11 28

EPHESIANS 2 10

1 PETER 5 8

PSALM 147 3

MATTHEW 6 27/8

JOHN 16 33

ROMANS 12 2

XIII

Fear and Courage

UNRAVELING

'F'ear is healthy and natural at times. A little bit of fear will keep you alive and humble. In the same way that a little bit of electricity keeps your heart beating, while too much will end your life. Albeit not normally aware of it, fear profusely influences and imbalances our perception of events that happen around us. These lopsided interpretations typically result in two extremes: overly and unnecessarily guarded, or conversely, an alarming eagerness to engage in hazardous activities. To surmount this hindrance, knowledge is necessary but does not operate in seclusion. We must act on this knowledge and practice employing actions that rewire the brain, which in turn feeds our knowledge. This cycle of gaining and applying knowledge can be likened to the continual broadening and deepening root system of a tree.

When discussing fear, we are not simply talking about curious phobias like Coulrophobia (fear of clowns), Dendrophobia (fear of trees), or even Pogonophobia (fear of beards). We are specifically addressing fears such as separation, rejection, humiliation, and failure. I would be remiss though if I didn't briefly mention the number one horror of Americans that surpasses death: Glossophobia – the fear of public speaking.

I have had to speak to audiences quite frequently over the past few years and I'll let you in on a little secret, I absolutely dread it. But, in deconstructing the fear of public speaking though, we find a few core elements of fear itself residing within insecurities. Not knowing the result (will they make fun of me, what if I say something stupid) illustrates two sides to the coin of fear: unknown outcome and suspected consequence.

Before we dig too deep, let's explore the physiology of fear for a moment. Fear is a response that starts with the brain, in a region called the amygdala. This region is responsible for experiencing and processing emotions and is part of the *limbic system* – our behavioral CPU. An example of how this system works would be to imagine yourself taking an autumn stroll through the woods. Your feet rustle the already fallen leaves on the path while your eyes scan the canopy above, appreciating the reds, oranges, and yellows. Noticing two squirrels frolic through the canopy, your thoughts turn over memories from previous holidays with family members, when suddenly your reminiscing is interrupted. You hear a very distinct and agitated rattling near your foot. A sound you have possibly heard before in real life or on The Crocodile Hunter. Except, in this case, this feisty Shelia ain't a beaut' (We miss you, Steve Irwin).

The most peculiar aspect of the amygdala though is its primary role in memory formation. Which begs the question, if the component of the brain that is responsible for experiencing fear also has a main role in memory encoding, what does that say about the design of fear? By all accounts, it would need to be based on an event that has occurred in the past with a possibility of happening again in the future. So, to cut to the chase, fear is closely tied to memory, as well it should be.

Since the main focus of this book is recovery, we will now recalibrate and look at some of the fears that keep individuals in the bondage of addiction. Starting at the top and working consecutively down the list they are the fear of not having the willpower to do it, boredom, the possibility of relapse, the fear of change, and lastly, the fear of feeling. Fear controls you if you do not learn to control it. But learning to control it will take some time, practice, and faith.

This commentary on fear-based control is not a new perspective on the topic, nor is it a finding that a branch of psychology has stumbled upon over the many years of practicing their craft. It was originally stated more expertly when the New Testament was written:

… through fear of death were subject to lifelong slavery.

Hebrews 2:15b

The reason it appears that we are doing so much work on the front end of this chapter is that we have a promise that comes in an undecorated, two-lettered word. It will require our full attention and I do not want to provide supporting documentation once we arrive at our destination. When speaking about this promise, an extraordinary feeling will arise, that of courage. Courage, that chooses to act even though you feel fear, the resolve of the character to stand up and step forward in the face of the unknown.

CULTURE OF FEAR

At the time of writing this edition, we have been living through a popular culture of fear for quite a while now. I grew up in the 80s and it appears fear has exponentially snowballed since then. Parental worries of razor blades in

Halloween candy and the institution of matriarchal laws like making sure you are home when the streetlights come on, have been replaced with concerns that your six-year-old is getting too much screen time or finding out on the way to school that their laptop wasn't charged the night before.

Transparently though, I'm not sure if it was the culture, me being a child or if parents just weren't the hypochondriacs we have become today. Or there is another possibility, that fear has evolved to meet the times. I wish I could ask my parents if they ever worried about me riding my bike down the street. Because the thought of letting my kids pedal down that same road terrifies me now. However, though, I realize there is a chance I am just a little too disconnected from my children's generation to know how to empathize, properly. Regardless, the landscape has changed dramatically. When I was young, we were forced to conspire and MacGyver ways to get in trouble – it wasn't necessarily at our fingertips. Back in my day, we had to walk uphill both ways in the snow just to hunt for something mischievous to get into. Nowadays, trouble comes looking for kids, with every notification bell.

What is for certain though, is our level of uninterrupted connectedness, the deluge of popular opinion, and the 24-hour ad nauseam news cycle has incurred a spiritual debt in the form of emotional fatigue and mass neurosis. Has society really changed that much, or are we just more aware of the chaos? While this isn't structured to be a commentary on the current state of affairs, it does illustrate the difficulty of sifting out origins and interpretations of fear – where did it come from and what are we doing about it.

During my time, America has weathered the Challenger explosion, Y2K, the Mayan Calendar, multiple shootings, 9/11, pandemics, and the saturation of political theater and media rhetoric. As we progress through life and begin to stash some years under our belt, our definition of fear naturally matures. As children, most kids have an overactive imagination and come to fear what lurks underneath the bed. But some childhoods were littered with terrifying memories of slamming doors, heavy footsteps, loud arguments, and flashing lights. As we age though, childhood fears of boogeymen in closets give way to adult fears such as losing a job or a loved one or a routine check-up.

The Old Testament uses the Hebrew word arats (pronounced *aw-rats*) for fear. Arats characteristically means trembling dread. And how we either react or respond to this word is what reinforces its effects or removes its power entirely. Fear can and will render you useless and paralytic if you do not approach it with the courage to overcome the mental inertia required to create momentum against it.

Courage on the other hand comes from the Hebrew word amats (pronounced *aw-mats*), which means to be alert, steadfastly minded, and established. This word isn't about tiptoeing on the line of being self-assured or cocky, it is based on a measure of trust in God and having faith in Him and what He is capable of. Courage is bred through obedience to God and our understanding of His faithful character. We demonstrate courage based on our comprehension of His love. We live *with* courage.

PROMISES

Now that our framework is constructed, we have one verse and one word to focus on. The main characters of this verse are once again the Israelites, and the context is that they have just fled Egypt. However, their leader Moses has died. They have been wandering around in the wilderness for forty years and they are now being commanded by a new leader named Joshua to go into a land that is occupied and take control and ownership of it.

These are the same Israelites who previously complained to Moses that they wanted to return to slavery in Egypt. Over 600,000 grown men all whined about wanting fish and melons, instead of the manna God provided. (How bad was the moaning and complaining? Moses was so miserable that he actually prayed to God to go ahead and kill him so he wouldn't have to hear it anymore.)

Have I not commanded you? Be strong and courageous. Do not be frightened, and do not be dismayed, for the Lord your God is with you wherever you go.

Joshua 1:9

We could have chosen any single word or phrase to focus on for the remainder of our time with this topic; strong, courageous – literally anything else other than what we are going to concentrate on. Tactically though, I want to extrude one word that has most assuredly been overlooked because of its stealth-like ability to go undetected. This word is a promise – the word IS. The word the Lord chose to use was not 'maybe', 'sometimes', 'possibly' or 'was.' This word 'is', is so remarkable that it deserves an additional mention:

It *is* the Lord who goes before you. He will be with you; he will not leave you or forsake you. Do not fear or be dismayed.

Deuteronomy 31:8

IS is a promise. An active choice and a description of God's character. If you are seeking after what God wants you to do, if you profess Jesus as your savior, then cling to this promise. If sobriety, or doing without makes you sick to think about, if making apologies or seeking to reconcile or trying to do right when no one wants to encourage you makes you want to give up, if you are frightened by failure, be courageous. He *IS* with you.

DECIDE YOUR PATH

So, maybe courage for you is believing you will and can get through the day without giving in to the temptations of addiction. Maybe it is choosing to raise your hand when the pastor gives an altar call. Or perhaps courage is reaching out to someone in your time of need. Fear is especially powerful when you feel alone like you have no one to help you. It takes courage to take the first step on this quest. Do not let fear stand in your way of better. Enlist the help of others, because you are not alone on this journey. Satan loves to separate us from the rest of the flock at these times. Reach out for support and accept the probability that the forthcoming chapter of your life may be unknown and awkward, but God is with you.

Conversely, you may be on the other side of the fence. God has redeemed and strengthened you and now calls you to help others. Take the time to pray and make sure, but don't wander aimlessly in the wilderness for decades wondering if that is what He wants you to do. Be available for the lost and suffering, even if it felt like no one on this planet was there for you. Do not allow fear to become a barrier to pursuing the salvation of another person's soul. God wants to use you to encourage and help others for His glory and their eternity. Be courageous for them. Because they may be the very ones frozen on that leave-covered path in the woods, listening to the warning of the rattle get louder and louder.

Melia Huntley

> "Growing up, we never talked about drugs."

When I started using, I had no idea about drugs or the drug world. I left my husband, shortly after that I started dating someone who was an addict. Little did I know my entire life was about to change. After only using once I was addicted. Meth became my best friend. I lost my job of 13 years, sold everything I had of value, cashed in all my life insurance policies and 401k. I had no money, and nothing left so that relationship ended, and my drug use continued. I then started selling drugs to support my habit.

Seventeen years into my addiction I started using the needle. During the next three years, I found myself alone, homeless, I was raped, and soulless. I wanted to die. But God showed up and helped me turn my life around. He put people in my life that would walk with me every step of my journey. He restored my relationship with all my family and gave me new friends. He gave me back everything I lost and more. I now have a chance to help others that struggle with addiction. Recovery does not happen overnight. You will have good days and bad days through them all have faith, trust him and seek God in all you do.

Every word of God is flawless; he is a shield to those who take refuge in him.

Proverbs 30:5 (NIV)

JOHN 6 37

PHILIPPIANS 1 6

JOHN 14 18

1 PETER 2 11

MATTHEW 6 33

JEREMIAH 17 9

JOSHUA 1 9

GALATIANS 5 1

PROVERBS 11 2

MATTHEW 11 28

EPHESIANS 2 10

OV
ER
CO
ME

JEREMIAH 29 11

1 PETER 5 8

PSALM 147 3

MATTHEW 6 27

JOHN 16 33

ROMANS 12 2

XIV

Bitterness and Joy

HIDDEN WITHIN

Let's preemptively make everything awkward for everyone, shall we? How well do you claim to know your heart? Can you trust it to lead you correctly in every decision life may throw at you? How do you even know your answers to these questions are truthful and accurate? The honest answer, in any case, is: you can't. The heart is responsible for many wonderful and positively affirming endeavors like compassion, charity, sacrifice, and the many sappy love songs playing at meticulously planned weddings. As well, it is the source of many travesties that are equally weighty such as jealousy, divorce, and murder. The spiritual heart, as it turns out, is a phenomenal projector that betrays the character of whom it dwells within.

In unearthing this elusive criminal, we will use a fundamental engineering maxim and an analogy to illustrate the concept of *form follows function*. Picture a remote control. Its intended *function* – its utility – is to make interaction with a specific piece of technology easier for the user. For example, we will use the old trusty TV remote. A long, long time ago, televisions used to be these large consoles (basically a piece of furniture the size of a kitchen table that weighed in at hundreds of pounds. Not something as thin as this book that could be hung on a wall like a picture frame).

These consoles required the viewer to get up from the recliner, walk to the behemoth, and physically turn a knob to change the channel. During that dark time in technology, most children became de facto voice-operated remote controls for parents. Kids could change the channel, turn the volume up, and adjust the antennae.

Then someone came up with the ingenious idea of creating a device, attached via a cable, that eliminated the need for children (just kidding). But as you may suspect, this jump rope of an invention became a trip hazard, that frequently resulted in ripped-out wires and the spewing forth of profanities. This tiny oversight led to the next needed improvement – get rid of the wires. Infrared entered the scene and recliners and couches have never fully recovered from the sustained onslaught of overuse since that day.

But the function of the remote was to make it easier to interact with the TV. Shape and size are still pretty irrelevant and haven't experienced drastic changes over the years. But buttons, on the other hand, have proven to be an excellent candidate for continued evolution, because they are the main method for human interaction. This leads to the next point in our discussion, *form*.

If any of you grew up playing the original Nintendo, you may already know where I am going with this. Back in the day, Nintendo designers and manufacturers did not really appraise and appreciate the level of use their controller buttons would be subjected to. Instead of the button edges being rounded over, they came to a sharp square corner. Consequently, children across the world began experiencing a new ailment – controller thumb. If you were a dedicated gamer though, the blisters would eventually form calluses, thereby separating the men from the boys in the land of video games.

Comically, this ailment draws out the central theme of function – usage. And it not only drove the need to create a method for humans to interact with technology. Usage forced entire industries to re-evaluate how their products were being used. The evolution of the lowly remote shows form follows function to be a bedrock for product design, through its many years of progressive improvements – from manually changing channels, using a broomstick to adjust the bunny ears, child labor, glow in the dark numbers, to actual voice control. And if you really want to see how valuable this function is, conduct the social experiment of hiding someone's TV remote sometime. Regardless, the form and the function for anything will always be dependent on the application of it – not how you plan to use it, but how it is unquestionably being used.

Some pieces of knowledge we occasionally take for granted. We never really challenge why we have those beliefs and where did they come from. Furthermore, what function should these beliefs serve; do they improve my life somehow, does it provide safety, is it consistent and repeatable? Our spiritual heart is much the same. We know it is there and we know what it is supposed to do, but don't really know how to interact with it and what steps we need to take for it to reach its full potential as God designed it.

Our application for this chapter will be a reiteration of a previous suggestion. For some, it will be the single heaviest possession they have had to carry around and subsequently, will also be the hardest one to lay down. So, trust this isn't going to be leisurely exercise. It is one thing to cover bitterness when life is going well, but a completely different matter when you have just been reminded of why your disdain for someone else was kindled in the first place.

A RELATIONAL HEART DISEASE

When the Hebrew word for *heart* (levav) is translated, it is done so to encompass the inner man, the mind, the will. It is the same idea for the Greek word (kardia) that Jesus uses in Luke 12:34, which translates to the inner thoughts and feelings. We can attribute this metaphysical concept for the heart to be the central part of us, the responsible component for generating much of who we are, how we perceive things, and what we do with life. Form, function, and application.

For where your treasure is, there will be your heart also.

Luke 12:34

The heart was created to generate compassion, mercy, care, and love; not hatred and strife (although it is certainly proficient and quite capable of the latter). It is intended to house the soul and the internal values of the person within whom it dwelt – the spirit. Additionally, as it turns out, we are completely incapable of judging another person's heart. Only God can discern what is in that knotted-up mess. We Watsons may venture a guess and imagine we have the deductive prowess of Sherlock Holmes, but not with any certain level of precision. Since we can't, this deficiency makes obtaining a correct diagnosis increasingly complicated. The doctor can't perform the surgery and be the patient all at the same time.

Bitterness is a relational heart disease. Therefore, it doesn't just manifest on its own, it is the diseased product of two independent parties. Spiritually, when a heart suffers from sepsis, it is no longer capable of guiding us reasonably and our decisions will become more reactionary. What may be a feeling of love one minute, can just as easily be transformed into hate the next one. It is dynamically equipped to evolve and mutate based on what we feed it and how we care for it. A diet based solely on projected expectations and fulfillment from other sinners mixed with impatience at having our demands met results in 'hangry' feelings, thoughts, and sentiments such as:

>> Don't these people see how much I have sacrificed and worked for this; how can they not care? I give up.

>> I'll show them. They will miss me when I am gone.

>> How could you God? How could you let life turn out this way?

>> Why did I trust you? I knew this was going to happen! You have hurt me for the last time. I'll never forgive you!

>> Over my dead body.

History has revealed that deductive observation needs to be the precursory effort when attempting to unpuzzle a mystery, rather than blind and unguided action. In this situation, we must derive the why what, and how of the disease to properly remedy it. In the example of our remote, the flow chart for troubleshooting its non-operation progresses from banging it against the palm of your hand, to changing the batteries, then fussing at whoever spilled chocolate milk on it (in that overly specific order). The heart is a little different though, we can't just arbitrarily rely on a potentially faulty set of steps.

For our hearts, we need to know the root cause, regardless of the form it takes or the symptoms it shows. The root cause originates from our interactions with others – the want to be accepted, feel valuable, be noticed, and appreciated. When those expectations aren't met, our feelings get hurt. We feel angry and rejected. Sometimes these emotions dissipate quickly, but depending on the offense and the offender, we may choose to wallow in our bitterness for an extended period. Wallowing promotes festering and further infection. That infection is commonly referred to as a grudge, and the only antibiotic available is forgiveness.

In attempting to translate this thought into something a little more spiritually deeper than a broken TV remote, I ask you to open your bibles and interact with scripture for a moment. Find Jeremiah 17. Start at verse 5 and read through verse 8. In these verses, God is describing the folly of trusting in man – the futility of trying to find value and appreciation from other people. Since bitterness is relational and does not operate in a vacuum, we shouldn't act surprised when other people fail at validating us. God's design does not function that way. We are trying to make it work in a manner that it was never intended to.

The heart is deceitful above all things, and desperately sick; who can understand it?

Jeremiah 17:9

Likewise, God also describes the folly of trusting and pursuing the desires of one's own heart. As Proverbs 14:10 says, "The heart knows its own bitterness…" Why? Because it keeps track of the offenses. That's why in Paul's famous writing on what love is, found in 1 Corinthians 13 (NIV), he penned "love does not keep a record of wrongs." But the heart does in fact keep a tally of the crimes and the acceptable payment expected. And until that payment has been satisfied, interest accrues, maturing into a debt that can never be repaid. Unforgiveness becomes a financial mystery that leaves the bookkeeper scratching their head wondering why their ledgers aren't balanced. It is not the actual offense, but the emotional residue the debt has left behind.

However, in Jeremiah chapter 17 verses 7 and 8, God describes what it is like to trust in Him – to joy. Joy is not happiness, where happiness is based on acceptable circumstances and favorable situations. Happiness is fleeting. It ebbs and flows based on surroundings and events we normally can't control. Joy is not based on your bank account or how much your spouse approves of you. Joy is peaceful contentment and ease of the soul. It is always in development and isn't dependent on the world to sustain it. It is a confidence in God being who He says He is – in control and not subject to change His mood – like we are.

These things I have spoken to you, that my joy may
be in you, and that your joy may be full.

John 15:11

This type of joy is found in Jesus and it is a peace that guards your heart. I am aware of how natural it is to create a faulty yardstick to measure what we want to believe will bring us joy. This conditional standard says I will only be happy if this specific event occurs. This standard screams out *if I can only secure that promotion I have worked so hard for, if this person will finally give me the time of day, if I can get that new truck, if I will only try a little harder, happiness is around the corner!*

It is when we chase the aforementioned sources of 'happiness', do we find ourselves yielding to temptation. Choosing to relent and satisfy these temporary desires and impulses is what is responsible for the subtraction of true joy. The existence of this spiritual arithmetic surfaces when we pander to temptation, thereby losing our joy, and consequently leading to the dissipation of our peace. All because we desired our happiness instead of God's joy.

Mankind has spent much of its existence trying to offset this equation but to no avail. Attempting to interject worldly variables, humanity has only managed to find inconclusive solutions, plagued by polarity and bastardized imbalances. Frustratingly, our quest to find a suitable and permanent replacement for God has only produced failure and is a reminder of the futile experiments. Conclusively, joy is not a human cause, it is a divine effect.

And the peace of God, which surpasses all understanding, will guard your hearts and your minds in Christ Jesus.

Philippians 4:7

It may be somewhat necessary at this juncture to prepare you for the upcoming application. This will not be a sprint to the finish line. Rather, it will be more necessary to take the first step knowing it will be a marathon. Giving up ownership of debts you have collected from others is difficult. Please recognize the desire behind the request, to help free you of burdens and any further damage incurred on your behalf. We are a hurting people, and it takes a strong person to take the preliminary step toward securing joy, especially if you are the one who has been hurt. Giving up ownership of debt takes a step of faith in something greater than our feelings and more valuable than the violation. This is only possible when you:

Have faith in God, not your feelings.

TECHNICAL SUPPORT

There are many moments during recovery and your walk with God that make absolutely no sense in the day-to-day struggles. As we progress down the road of redemption, we are occasionally provided insight for a portion of these moments. Sometimes, we go home empty-handed. God is not obligated to disclose why He does what He does. Over time, experiences confirm His truth to be in fact, truth. Our interpretations naturally expand and evolve during this maturing process, but His truth never changes. Instead, we grow to fathom the truth more deeply because we are eagerly employing it. This is implemented through the forms of obedience and faith. These two forms allow our heart to function as it was designed to and provides us the means to undertake the final stage – troubleshooting.

Ask yourself, "What has robbed me of my joy?" Pay close attention to the attitude of your heart as offenses are brought forward. Is it too soon, things a little too touchy, just can't right now? Being objectively receptive is an outstanding step in learning how to discern your heart state. Do you find yourself justifying feelings or emotional reactions to past hurts? Are you fast-forwarding past certain memories or are you getting stuck in repetitive loops? Do you find yourself eager to do what you can to repair the relationship, or are the differences just so great there is no possibility for reconciliation? Is now just not the right time? What is preventing forgiveness from happening?

To give some sense of proportion, what we are attempting to do (on a much smaller scale) is to mimic the same forgiveness Jesus showed to His accusers and us on the cross. He was willing to die to right our wrongs. He was willing to die to reconcile us to an eternity with Him in heaven (the Christ-follower's ultimate reason for joy). He was willing to lay aside whatever debt it was and pay it on our behalf, all because the relationship was that important to Him. Since our Savior and Creator chose to forgive,

We must choose to forgive.

Tara Escobar

> "My walk with the Lord began many years ago as a child and young adult. I attended church on and off throughout my life on my own."

However, I didn't truly surrender myself to the Lord until Fall 2019 at the age of 30. That's when everything I knew about my life, who I was, and who Jesus Christ is, changed.

A certain guy and I have known each other since the 7th grade, long-time friends. As adults, we reconnected again when he was newly released from prison for the 3rd time in August 2018. He was 28 and I was 29. I was aware he'd struggled with addiction and had a lengthy record of time served spanning almost 10 years. He was clean then and promised his days of heroin, meth, pills, marijuana, and breaking the law was over. He said once, "I thought I'd been to hell before, until this last time in prison due to my addiction. I found out hell had a basement, and I'm never going back." He then followed that up with "I love you, and I'll never trade you for drugs." Uneducated and inexperienced in the world of addiction, I blindly trusted his addiction was in full, permanent remission. Little did I know, the devil himself would soon return to drag us both to the "crawl space" beneath Hell's basement. This is where I met the enemy of our God face to face for the first time. It was only then that I finally, truly called upon the Lord to bring me to salvation as a believer in Christ and deliver me from evil.

In September 2018, we began a fairy tale romance with the kind of love you pray for but only ever see in movies. We became inseparable; he was my best friend, my forever, my happy ending. Nothing would ever come between us, or so I thought. A few months into our relationship he relapsed. I watched addiction rip my best friend and love of my life apart one long grueling hour, day, week, and month at a time. My life was no longer mine to live - it had become a by-product of his addiction. After enduring months of endless lies, manipulation, theft, paranoia, and arguing, I was mentally, emotionally, financially, and physically drained.

Eventually, I made the hardest decision of my life, in order to save his life. I pressed charges against him – totaling 33 counts of felony, making him a 4th time convicted felon. In October 2019, he was sentenced to prison, and my life changed forever that day. I realized then and there, I could not clean up the wreckage of my life and broken heart alone. There was no way out of this disaster without God as the center of my life. It was time I surrender and give my life to the Lord 100%. Because I knew His way was the only way to salvation. And that's exactly what I did...

Today, I am a witness of the Lord's work in my life through the addiction in that relationship. Since he was sentenced, I became a volunteer for BRPJM (Blue Ridge Prison and Jail Ministries), ministering to women inmates and sharing my testimony. I spend every Monday with Back on Track Addiction Ministries in Family Support strengthening my knowledge and understanding of addiction at its core as a disease. My healing and recovery continue on while serving other families and active addicts in need of support, with God as my pilot. I give back to the community as a faithful Christian and dedicate a large part of my life to serve the mission field of addiction. I find my front-row seat at Ebenezer Baptist Church of Hendersonville every Sunday, thankful and thirsty for the Lord's word.

After forgiving the events of the past and in the process of growing my faith and rebuilding my relationship with the Lord, I was Baptized on December 6, 2020. My best friend was released after 18 months served and is sober, healthy, and happy today. He continues to be successful on his road to recovery by God's grace every day. He has surrendered himself to the Lord as a born-again Christian and we have rekindled our relationship together as a faithful Christian couple. We are stronger than ever serving the Lord, and on the mission field of addiction together. Glory be to God for all we have been, all we are and have yet to be.

My brothers, if anyone among you wanders from the truth and someone brings him back, let him know that whoever brings back a sinner from his wandering will save his soul from death and will cover a multitude of sins.

James 5:19-20

OVERCOME

PHILIPPIANS 1 6

JOHN 6 37

JOHN 14 18

1 PETER 2 110

MATTHEW 6 33

JEREMIAH 17 9

JOSHUA 1 9

JEREMIAH 29 11

GALATIANS 5 1

PROVERBS 11 2

MATTHEW 11 28

EPHESIANS 2 10

1 PETER 5 8

PSALM 147 3

MATTHEW 6 27

JOHN 16 33

ROMANS 12 2

XV

Hubris and Humility

A BREEDING GROUND

Pride. Ah yes, the sun rises and sets at our command. We are the center of the universe because no one else is even remotely qualified for the job. Pride is genetically the grandfather of all sin once you whittle it down to the quick. But then again, the prideful person already knows this. While the onset of pride is subtle and deafening, the offset is responsible for producing foolish pupils. Pride encourages comparison and selfish expression. If you believe this to be dramatization, partake in the following rudimentary social experiment: go an entire day without referring to your achievements or voicing your opinions during conversations. (Hiding in bed for 24 hours doesn't count.)

With a multitude of quotes and verses of scripture that address pride, there is literally no shortage of literature on this matter – from Nietzsche to Solomon, Oedipus Rex to Jesus Christ. There is no longer a dispute of denomination or professional opinion. Everyone agrees, pride is an undesirable and repulsive quality… found in other people. But somehow, we find it tolerable and acceptable in ourselves. The reason we can pinpoint sin rather quickly in another person is because of our level of afflicted intimacy with it. The reason it feels familiar to us is because:

The sin in me recognizes the sin in you.

As mentioned back in the prologue, it has been quite an undertaking to translate a group meeting into a published work, let alone a personal edition. One of the components of the original class design was discussing a celebrity personality who had succumbed to one of the destructive reactions we covered. In this translation, I have removed the celebrity references because I did not want to inspire hearsay and risk missing the entire nucleus of the discussion. With that being said, I will note one observation regarding research and development. It was alarmingly difficult to find celebrities who had indeed recovered from addiction, as opposed to those who have expired as a consequence of it. Tragically, I believe this dire conclusion to be the effect of the topical concern we discuss in this chapter.

The problem with pride is that the one suffering from this condition is never wrong, which means it will be a struggle for them to be humble. They sincerely believe they are right deep within their heart. Now it is easy to be on the other side of the keyboard and point the finger at all the people whom I believe are prideful, especially if they disagree. Even though we are violently aware of the pride in others, we somehow exhibit blissful ignorance when undergoing the same diagnosis and treatment options with ourselves.

A QUESTION OF PERSPECTIVE

The word hubris is a sophisticated way to describe excessive pride, self-confidence, and arrogance. The Bible refers to individuals with this character trait as *stiff-necked*. So, for the duration of this chapter, hubris, pride, and arrogance can be used interchangeably. In *Mere Christianity*, CS Lewis calls pride "the great sin." Albert Einstein famously said, "the only thing more dangerous than ignorance is arrogance." While God does not have a sliding scale when it comes to sin, we need to be particularly mindful of the dangers and by-products stemming from pride: anger, bitterness, rejection, burden, exhaustion, envy, disappointment, gossiping and comparing. While this is not an exhaustive list, we will briefly occupy ourselves with the last one.

When we compare, we begin looking up and down the food chain. Who is doing better and who is doing worse? While looking up the food chain could generate inspiration, it usually provokes envy. Whereas looking down the food chain should prompt compassion and generosity, it usually gives rise to pride. When we initiate the sport of comparison, we begin to notice the shortcomings of certain people on one hand and posture the deadly stance of self-importance on the other. Choosing to participate in this activity, we become dismissive of others by talking down to them in belittling manners, and conversely, jumping on the bandwagon to play the game of one-ups-man-ship with those we feel inferior to. All sorts of gifts can breed arrogance: houses, money, cars, job, spouse, looks, talents, even knowledge. Unconsciously, we divulge the areas we feel are the most impressive by comparing to them the most often. Whether bragging or envying, byproducts of pride will always find a way to ooze out.

When pride comes, then comes disgrace, but with the humble is wisdom.

Proverbs 11:2

Notice the wording of this verse, Solomon says *when* pride comes, not *if* pride comes. When God asked him what did he want, he was especially specific in 1 Kings 3. Solomon requested "a discerning heart..." to rule God's people. With that knowledge, we can only logically assume Solomon was well equipped to observe and report the many motivations for why we humans do what we do since he could accurately and divinely deduce human behavior and action. As wise as Solomon was, he still had his faults – further verifying that wisdom is not just about the accumulation of knowledge but requires action as well.

Back to our main verse, notice the word he uses after the first comma, *then*. This is a cause-and-effect statement, a formula. Pride consequentially leads to disgrace: the perpetual remorse of conscience. What goes up, must come down. The book of Proverbs is laden with this type of structured advice for living a godly life. And, as it turns out, Solomon had quite a bit to say about the progression of this dis-ease: pride comes before disgrace (11:2), a haughty spirit before the fall (16:18), pride before destruction (18:12), pride brings a person low (29:23), and many more.

STILL A STUDENT

Look at the last section of our main verse, "but with the humble is wisdom." This is the understood contrast and within it lies the heart of addressing pride. We have the negative consequence to partially reinforce against pride, but we need the positive reward to move from discipline to growth. We, in other words, choose to open ourselves up to instruction. While pride makes people unteachable, humility makes us ready, willing, and able students.

Words like humility sound repulsive and leave a bad taste in our mouth when we say them, don't they? It is because humility goes directly against our self-based nature and culture. You don't have to teach a child how to be selfish, it is one of the attributes we seem to be born with. Instinctively, as we get older, we hone our cleverness and learn to disguise this nasty little character trait. After a while of performing this act, it takes a conscious effort of the will to experience actual humility. That is if we can resist the urge to tell everyone about our benevolent actions. But once we come to Christ, we acknowledge that we don't know everything, can't do it all, and life doesn't revolve around us as we thought. A humbling lesson we will continue to learn the rest of our lives in many different forms, especially if we continue to rebel against the Teacher.

Incurably, we will always fight against being self-based organisms. The tendency in our spiritual walks is to exhibit humility in the early stages, but eventually, give way to pride as we grow further away from our moment of salvation. This subtle demolition of our spiritual house mainly occurs unintentionally, resembling something closer to a vine creeping up the brickwork more so than a 15,000-pound wrecking ball. We stop looking at the log in our own eye and start looking at specks in the eyes of others. When we do this, we are no longer focusing on our growth, but projecting our comparison onto others, because we have elected our self to be the apex of righteousness and God's gift to all the other slackers and nincompoops. We no longer need to learn anything, because frankly, we already know-it-all – or at least more than the other guy.

(As a constricting by-product of this attitude, pride kinks the water hose of grace a little too much. Predominately, humility – the opposite of hubris – is a necessary catalyst for good to not only flow into your life but out from it.)

DON'T SIT AT THE HEAD OF THE TABLE

As always, Jesus gave us a walking model of humility and its value in His Word. For example, when He washed the disciples' feet at the last supper, found in John chapter 13. During dinner, He put Himself in a position of servitude and washed their feet. (Historically, feet have always been regarded as rather unpleasant. During the days of Jesus, merely adding up the facts will paint an authentically profound representation of the act He performed. Mostly everyone walked to wherever they were going, sandals were the standard footwear, and the roads were also used by animals hauling wagons – recall any parade you have seen where horses were present, and what the road looked like afterward – feet could get pretty funky. Since our feet carry us everywhere and "run to evil" (Isaiah 59:7), periodically they need to be washed. Pride says, "I'm not washing them, they are not dirty." It becomes a repugnant stench we are incapable of removing, only our Lord and Savior can.) What is especially effective for us and our topic, is that in His position of humility, He gave us an illustration of our need for Him. He put Himself in that position to do what needed to be done. When He says "The servant is not above the master" it means that when we only consider ourselves, we become our own master and everyone else becomes our petty servants (including Jesus), which is completely out of alignment with God's design.

We ought to ambitiously serve others, instead of looking for others to serve us. For most addicts, we have been serving ourselves for a large portion of our lives. In the past, we more than likely defined and formed relationships based on utility. We took much from our family and friends when we reduced their existence down to tools and view them as a means to an end. Since it takes an intentional act of humility to jumpstart the process, a little awareness exercise might benefit us. We will start with two questions and then a final request. Bear with me, we are traveling to a very specific destination.

1. *Why* has He given you these gifts?
     I am certain that God did not bless us with talents for us to turn our back on Him and bathe in the perfume of self-confidence (or conversely, wreak

of camel dung between our toes). Routinely, gifts can, and often do, become idols and instruments for self-worship – not at all what their intended usage was when they were given. Gifts and talents are meant to glorify the One who gave them, by reflecting the Giver and benefiting others. Granted, we can enjoy them as well, but they should not be the alpha and omega of life.

2.   *How* are you using them?

The fact that we have been given something does not imply that it is being used, let alone being used correctly. I can confirm this fact just by observing the kids at the house. We buy them toys and they become hammers. We give them tools and they become guns. Has God blessed you with an artistic skill, a beautiful voice, athletic ability, a mechanical mind, a wonderful family? How are they being used and to what effect are you using them?

And finally, as promised, our destination. The following request is based upon a practice I have recently adopted when giving my testimony. I will admit ahead of time, it may feel awkward and out of place. An important lesson learned since I began speaking to groups is that most people will forget what they have heard in a matter of a few days (if you're lucky and managed to make an impression). Most often though, life will come rushing back and they will forget the majority of everything you said as soon as they walk out of the door. But what I want to accomplish when giving my testimony is to provide people with something they can walk out with and have with them. They will eventually forget they have it until they are scrolling through pictures on their phone one day and happen to pass by it. I humbly ask that you take a moment and do this, in the same manner I asked them to.

Open your phone and go to the camera, set it to take a picture of yourself, and then lay it to the side for a moment. Begin this exercise by closing your eyes and recall the place that Jesus found you. Think about the environment and try to remember as many details as you possibly can. What day was it? Was the sun shining or was it raining? Was it morning or evening? What holiday was nearby? What were you wearing; your slippers, a pair of ripped-up jeans, your favorite hoodie, a suit? Where were you; at church, in jail, a hospital bed, perhaps your living room? What smells were present? What sounds do you remember; a dripping faucet, yelling in the background, a song, sobbing... silence?

After you have recalled the spatial details, I ask you to attempt to dredge up the emotional memories of that moment. What else was going on in your life; was it chaotic? What led you to this point where you found yourself at? Loss of a job, a loved one, an arrest, a troubling diagnosis, an overdose? What burdens, hurts, pain, shame, and sadness were you carrying around? Were you beaten down, suffocated, broken? It may be painful but remember these feelings and the crushing spiritual weight you experienced before He came into your life.

Now, re-capture that moment when Jesus embraced you and came into your heart. The elation the moment you felt forgiveness, the acceptance, the hope, the tears that fell when those suffocating burdens were lifted. What did that moment feel like? Seize that feeling and hold on to it. Now, open your eyes and take a picture of yourself.

That is humility.

Chazeray Jackson

"In May 2012, I found myself awoken by car horn while behind the wheel of my fiancée's car, inches away from a head-on collision."

I could have killed myself and the person driving the other vehicle. I turned the wheel to the right and crashed into a wooden gate. I remember getting arrested and was taken to jail shortly after for driving while under the influence of alcohol.

I remember being in that jail cell, thinking about the emotional baggage that was heavy on my soul. I define emotional baggage as "life's traumas and dramas that go unresolved." I grew up in an unstable environment and developed a belief system built upon low self-esteem and poor social skills. This environment was further influenced by drugs, alcohol, domestic abuse, and poor leadership.

The Apostle Paul tells us in Romans 12:1, "Do not conform any longer to the pattern of this world but be transformed by the renewing of your mind." My fiancée Amy played a huge role in helping me renew my mind. I remember the following week or so Amy and I visited my lawyer. After Amy and I got back in the car, Amy told me that he recommended that she get away from me. I remember asking her, "why don't you leave me?" She was God's echo by saying,

"I see something in YOU that you don't see in yourself."

I believe God used her to help renew my mind and remind me of my true potential. I knew a change needed to happen. I enrolled in a 42-day rehabilitation program. The program helped me overcome the emotional baggage I was carrying, and I discovered firm solutions to my problems. I became a true follower of Jesus Christ during the journey through this program.

As of 2021, I have not had a drink of alcohol in eight years and counting. I am married to the most wonderful woman in the world, we have two beautiful daughters, and they all have been by my side since the beginning.

My life's journey as a husband, father, teacher in physical therapy, and youth leader is to break the generational curse of "you are a product of your environment." I strive to encourage others despite their circumstances or where they come from. We all are gifted differently to make a difference. I am passionate about helping future leaders harness the greatness inside of them and serve in their area of gifting led by God.

Lastly consider this: "Let your light shine before men, that they may see your good works, and glorify your Father which is in heaven." (Matthew 5:16)

OVERCOME

JOHN 6 37
PHILIPPIANS 16
JOHN 14 18
JEREMIAH 17 9
JOSHUA 19
MATHEW 6 33
1 PETER 2 11
JEREMIAH 29 11
GALATIANS 51
PROVERBS 11 2
MATHEW 11 28
EPHESIANS 2 10
1 PETER 58
PSALM 147 3
JOHN 16 33
MATTHEW 6 27
ROMANS 12 2

XVI

Anger and Clarity

MIOSIS

One of the momentary and problematic effects of anger is that it severely clouds your vision. This clouding blinds you to reality and impedes decision-making. But usually, we find this out after the fact – after we have cooled down and realized, maybe we shouldn't have said or done that. Then you get the humbling and not so honorable duty of making amends. Which is not a fun spot to find yourself in, and if you frequent it too often, you'll find yourself casually purchasing an overpriced townhouse there, even though you know you can't afford it. But the schools are nice, and the neighbors seem friendly. No matter how much you think you can keep the different areas of your life compartmentalized and quarantined from anger, it will eventually spill over just like every other sin. We assume we can hide it when needed, until one day it outgrows the closet and bursts into the dining room like a rabid St. Bernard when you are having dinner one evening with the nice couple from down the street.

There is a strange and cathartic stage, if you will, much like the first real moments of sobriety when the scales have fallen off your eyes and you start to perceive life with an awkward clarity. You now see obstructions that you didn't know were there previously. You notice signs that you never paid attention to in the past, mostly regarding yourself and your actions. This nauseating phase can be likened to waking up one morning to a precise beam of sunlight that has found its way through the tiniest of cracks between the bedroom curtains, landing strategically upon your eyelids. The slight twinge of pain produced from the constricting of pupils signals evasive actions are required. Twisting and writhing in attempts to somehow clamp your eyes tighter, but it is too late. The sadistic ray was broken into an obnoxious show tune rendition of "Put on a Happy Face."

The conflict that transpires during this time of sober lucidity – when you are faced with your reflection and start to see who you are and what you have become – can be contrasted between darkness and light. Darkness being wrought by anger and light being operated by clarity. Darkness being who we once were and light, who we were meant to be. This light may be foreign and initially discomforting, but once you get used to it, it makes going back into the darkness all the more repulsive.

Again Jesus spoke to them, saying, "I am the light of the world. Whoever follows me will not walk in darkness, but will have the light of life."

John 8:12

OPENING A CAN OF WORMS

Idiotically, I opened a can of worms the first time teaching this specific lesson when I asked the class what made them angry? Which has led to including an explicit disclaimer: It is not up to me or another person to validate or invalidate your anger. All I can do is guide you to scripture. I do not have the spiritual discernment to judge the motives or heart of another person, I can't even judge my own heart adequately. I can, however, whitewash and excuse with the best of them. And if justification were an Olympic event, I would be the Usain Bolt of the pack.

This disclaimer leads us to an expected detour in this study: righteous anger and our personal point of view. The reason for the non-involvement with other peoples' anger is due to the overabundance of subjective information – or lack of objective information, to be more accurate. Attempting to parse out aspects such as point of view, my personal history with the subject, and a myriad of other variables is an exhausting exercise in futility. So, instead of demonstrating the definition of insanity, scriptural references are sprinkled throughout this chapter to help guide you towards a gospel answer regarding the validation of anger.

Know this, my beloved brothers: let every person be quick to hear, slow to speak, slow to anger; for the anger of man does not produce the righteousness of God.

James 1:19-20

While anger is a part of life, there is such a thing as righteous anger and indignation, but we ought to be especially careful not to automatically chalk up outbursts as such. Aggressively and defensively, we find ourselves justifying our bouts of anger, regardless of the scenario. The most convicting way to determine the motivation is to query if you get angry at *everything* else God gets angry about, or only a few specific issues? Matters that make you upset, may not even register with me. Likewise, there are a few personal gremlins I have a history with that become burdens when they happen to me or witness them happening to others (not in the superhero or even anti-hero variety, but more so in the manner of a super-annoyed villain.) This means, I am not necessarily angry with them for offending God, but rather I am offended (honestly though, *annoyed* may be a more appropriate description). Once again revealing the sliding scale we use to measure issues that do not necessarily lend themselves to being gauged in such a manner. As with the comparative ordinal scale, we can only assert that something is greater than or less than. Some issues are of greater importance to certain people, while the same matters are less pressing to others. This ambiguity is commonly referred to as the deadly gray area known as preference.

Be angry and do not sin; do not let the sun go down on your anger, and give no opportunity to the devil.

Ephesians 4:26-27

The overarching debate is not *if* you get angry, but more so why do you get angry. And accordingly, how do you handle anger – does it take control of you, or have you mastered it? When anger strikes, it is often in our weakest areas and during our most vulnerable moments. And everyone else seems to be standing around, with nothing better to do, other than observe how we react to the provocations. Whether resulting from intentional prodding, consolidated frustration, or un-rehabilitated hurt, reactive anger leaves a lasting impression. It is during these opportunities that others get a chance to see Jesus in me, instead of the 'me' within me. A prospect I habitually fail at the older I get and the more people I come into contact with.

THE ROARING LION

Agreed, there are so many different applications and alternative directions we could have ventured with this scripture. Please understand, what I am going to focus on in this passage is not the only truth there, as with all scripture. Other jewels can be mined out and polished such as predatorial patterns and generational sin. But for the intent of this study, I want to define a few words and tease out a logically implied observation of the outcome and subsequent effects when we instinctively react to troubling situations with fury and outrage.

Be sober-minded; be watchful. Your adversary the devil prowls around like a roaring lion, seeking someone to devour.

1 Peter 5:8

Since anger disorients us, let's start with the last word first. *Devour* means to consume entirely, by any and all means necessary – "ate up." Anger is typically built up and compiled over the course of many situations and perceived offenses. It develops as we ruminate over it, talk about it, and get worked up about the event. We become ticking time bombs due to stuffing and find it hard to contain emotions during the bottling process – firing passive-aggressive warning shots across the bow of those who have offended. Like Chunk so elegantly expressed in *The Goonies*, "That's all I can stand, and I can't stand no more."

The author, Peter, was one of Jesus' disciples. Boisterous and bold, he is also the one that habitually stuck his foot in his mouth and actually cut a soldier's ear off when they came to arrest Jesus. But out of the twelve, he appeared to be the most passionate, so when he appeals for us to be *sober-minded* and *watchful*, it may be in our best interest to urgently take notice. This earnest plea construes a conscious choice – not a subconscious reaction. It is a quality and a description of that choice – not a feeling – but rather an intentional call for alertness. For a hands-on example, it may be methodically wiser to walk away from an argument and starve it to death, as Proverbs 17:14 says "The beginning of strife is like letting out water, so quit before the quarrel breaks out." So much of the process of gaining clarity is fulfilled when we dwell on scripture, an intentional choice to apply biblical guidance instead of scratching the itch of vengeance.

Repay no one evil for evil, but give thought to do what is honorable in the sight of all. If possible, so far as it depends on you, live peaceably with all. Beloved, never avenge yourselves, but leave it to the wrath of God, for it is written, "Vengeance is mine, I will repay, says the Lord."

Romans 12:17-19

DREDGING THE BOTTOM

In a bit of value-added transparency regarding anger, I allowed many of the inflicted wrongs in my younger years to generate feelings of anger and detachment not only throughout childhood but well into my adult years. This anger resulted in self-imposed isolation and the systematic devaluing of other human beings. Because of allowing the trauma and anger to devour me, I became a drastically different person than what I imagined God designed me to be originally. Much of how I handled anger originated from my misunderstanding of God and directing misplaced hatred toward Him. I attributed the childhood rejection, neglect, and abuse to signify that He approved of it and even orchestrated it. Handling anger wrongly cost me years I will never get back and relationships that unfortunately cannot be reconciled on this side of heaven.

The topic of anger can best be illustrated through a principle of fluid mechanics known as displacement. Archimedes (basically the same equivalent of Albert Einstein, except in late 200 BC) was respected for his many contributions to science. Most notably, he first observed the principle of buoyancy, via a rather specific set of circumstances. He was requested by the king of Syracuse to determine if a newly made crown was indeed made of pure gold or faked, as many suspected. In a roundabout way, the discovery of displacement – and subsequently the authenticity of the crown – was made accidentally during a bath. This discovery led to the historical (and possibly anecdotal) account of a naked Archimedes running through the streets exclaiming "Eureka!" (I have found it!)

Archimedes stumbled upon the solution one day, by noticing how much water spilled out of the tub when he got in it to bathe. The space his body took up forced a certain volume of water up and out. Displacement occurs, not so much because of the weight of an object, but more the volume and surface area of it. This is the same principle that allows the 657,019 ton (almost 1.5 billion pounds) oil tanker once known as the *Seawise Giant* to float, and not sink to the bottom of the ocean – although it may be responsible for high tide inching a little further up the beach.

I introduce this perspective to unify a concluding thought on the topic of anger. The fact that anger is a volumetric reaction (takes up a lot of real estate in our hearts and minds), we must appreciate the level of destruction this emotion is habitually responsible for. Attempting to avoid all sources of anger in life is impractical and unfeasible. However, we can govern the damage incurred when faced with walking through these spiritual briar patches by comprehending how much clarity and peace are displaced when anger cannonballs the pool of our hearts.

> But what comes out of the mouth proceeds from the heart, and this defiles a person. For out of the heart come evil thoughts, murder, adultery, sexual immorality, theft, false witness, slander.
>
> Matthew 15:18-19a

The main fulcrum is this, whatever we fill that pool with, is what is going to overflow. If we are collecting frustrations, annoyances, and hurts, how can we expect anything else to spill out? Understandably, but falsely so, we often believe that we can rectify issues in the same manner they were created. We cannot solve frustrations with anger, any more so than cleaning up spilled water, with more water. If you find yourself consistently erring on the side of anger as the go-to solution for 'unpleasant' situations, there is a chance that you are allowing yourself to be devoured. And this isn't a cartoonish caricature of two dopey buzzards sitting on top of a dried-up coyote carcass out in the desert as tumbleweeds ramble by. It is more akin to a starving lion with its head and blood-matted mane buried inside the ribcage of a gazelle, aggressively eating it from the inside out. Ravenously snapping sinew and bone, only pausing to catch a brief, gurgling breath until only fur and intestines remain.

We do not want to devour ourselves or others. Know that whatever the offense is, Jesus' death on the cross paid it – in full. This is an intense truth to absorb, especially when it appears God is not bringing justice to your situation. Rest in the resolute clarity that the offense has not been overlooked and there is a reason for the delay (not a green light to become a caped vigilante). We are all screwed up, and we are all in debt. We do not want to allow the devil to drive us to devour each other, any more than wanting to be devoured ourselves. Scan the horizon and stay alert.

OVERCOME

PHILIPPIANS 1 6

JOHN 14 18

JEREMIAH 17 9

JOHN 6 37

JOSHUA 1 9

1 PETER 2 11

MATTHEW 6 33

JEREMIAH 29 11

GALATIANS 5 1

PROVERBS 11 2

MATTHEW 11 28

EPHESIANS 2 10

1 PETER 5 8

PSALM 147 3

MATTHEW 6 27

JOHN 16 33

ROMANS 12 2

XVII

Self and Sacrifice

ANALOG VS. DIGITAL

Most, if not all New Year's resolutions are aimed at making us better versions of ourselves. Start that diet, work out more, learn a new language or give up smoking. Regardless of the want, sustained change is simply improbable without a measurable level of commitment to the cause. What may have been a good idea at the moment, is now relegated to obscurity because the individual lacked sincerity. We close out our study by covering the topic I believe to be the single most grueling biblical principle – not only to be aware of but to apply – the disease of the *self*. It is so intimidating that it was intentionally saved for last. While it may sound like I am exaggerating, (rest assured) there is literally no need for me to attempt to oversell this to you. Because every topic we have covered up to this point has merely been symptomatic of this specific internal disease.

For such a weighty subject, we must employ the use of an analogy. In this instance, we will use a framework built to compare electrical signals – digital and analog. A digital signal is either a 0 or 1. These signals are commonly referred to as part of a binary system. Think of digital as a coin having heads or tails, or a light switch that is either up or down. Many complex systems can be built from this architecture, because of the logic behind it. This logic is based on answering the question, "On or off?" This sort of argument occurs every moment of every day in our lives, just in different fashions. So, just as an experiment to illustrate the scale of this absurd magnitude, try to imagine all the decisions that took place inside your mind today up until the reading of this very sentence. Every one of those instances (once reduced down to a simple yes or no) are representative of digital logic.

In contrast, an analog signal is best described using the word *intensity* and measuring it on a scale of 0 to 10. Analog describes qualities like how loud the volume is, how fast a car is traveling, or the temperature reading on a mercury thermometer. The primary aspect of this type of signal is it is best observed over a period of time. Time duration affects our perception and interpretation of analog. Over time, analog signals tend to trend and equalize in one direction or the other, much like our lives and the choices we make, good or bad. Where digital is fixed, analog is fluid.

BINARY LOGIC
Congruous sacrifices demonstrate themselves over time in a chronological analog fashion. When we repeatedly choose something that we are willing to exchange for something else, we concede the product to be worth the payment. For example, eight hours a day for five days a week is the exchange of time and toil for a living wage plus benefits. This exchange is a form of sacrifice, one thing must be given up for something else. Some of these sacrificial areas are family, friends, employment, health, and reputation. These areas get sacrificed (to varying degrees) in normal daily life, well before we introduce a variable such as addiction to be factored into this transactional equation. Once again, we are faced with unearthing the concept of a species created and existing as a duality – spiritual and physical.

Jesus was quite clear on this truth when He said we "cannot serve two masters." Trying to serve the self and Christ at the same time is contrary to each other, the requirements are just too drastically different. This polar opposition is especially true when it comes to memories of who you used to be versus belief in who Jesus knows you can become. Once you accept Christ, your identity changes as well as your investment. In this regard, sacrifice addresses the issue of identity ownership as well.

This conundrum, as it appears to be, is presented as a simple choice, yet as complex as the analysis of patterns and trends. For us, this subject of sacrifice is merely an examination of the momentary ones and zeroes adding up to establish an analogic trend. Are we going to habitually serve ourselves or are we going to consistently serve Jesus?

A MOST LIKELY PREMISE

Since we are living in such an egocentric society, addressing this subject is not a simple assignment to conduct, that is, without stepping on some toes in the process. Understand my aim, I am not here to beat you up as stated previously. My goal is to help you live the Christ-centered life as best as possible and fill in some of the cracks that I have stepped in along the way while bumbling down the path.

In our anchor verse, we find Peter writing to God's people to remind them who they are and encourage them to continue striving towards righteousness. Granted, he is reminding them of who they used to be, but it is done so to inspire and motivate. It also serves as a dire warning and wake-up call to be aware of the all too easily ignored and discounted war that is being waged around us every day. In other words, he is coaching them to get their head in the game and quit staring at the dandelions on the infield.

> Once you were not a people, but now you are God's
> people; once you had not received mercy, but now
> you have received mercy. Beloved, I urge you as
> sojourners and exiles to abstain from the passions of
> the flesh, which wage war against your soul.

1 Peter 2:10-11

He is telling them "Yes, that is who you *used to be*, but that's not who you are now. You are worth more than what you have sold yourself for." He is trying to instill in them their true identity – God's people – not whatever desire the heart of the self may have at that moment. In Ephesians, Paul provides another angle to further solidify this disjunction of who we used to be and who we are now.

> And you were dead in the trespasses and sins in which
> you once walked, following the course of this world,
> following the prince of the power of the air, the spirit
> that is now at work in the sons of disobedience—
> among whom we all once lived in the passions of our
> flesh, carrying out the desires of the body and the
> mind, and were by nature children of wrath, like the
> rest of mankind.

Ephesians 2:1-3

What may seem like a sacrifice is nothing other than separation anxiety with the items we have found comfortable familiarity with, in this world. Since the world changes every minute, how can you expect to have any form of stability when your foundation is constantly shifting? I'm not downing the world; I'm saying our Father in heaven does not change. He is steadfast and the only one capable of bestowing a permanent and eternal identity. But we must choose which identity we want the most. The primary reason for this caution was stated by Jesus in Luke 9:62. "No one who puts his hand to the plow and looks back is fit for the kingdom of God." Additionally, this caution is provided by Solomon in Proverbs 26:11 as "a dog returning to his vomit, is the same as a fool who returns to his sin." One identity is simply too antagonistic to the other one. Attempting to live in both of them at the same time will tear you apart.

SELF OR SPIRIT?

This question is constantly being asked all the time, whether we know it or not. Are we sojourners and exiles, or are we still children of wrath? Every time you are faced with this question and answer it, you are providing a digital signal – a zero or a one, yes or no, good or bad. Over time, these digital signals will add to (or subtract from) a total composite based on the most consistent answer you provide, averaging your analog signal; do you gravitate more in this direction or that direction? Do you find yourself constantly reverting to who you used to be (slave to self) or do you find your actions aligning more with your new heavenly identity? This identity crisis is essentially a battle of attrition – who is going to be the last one standing when the smoke clears?

The apparent victor of this war will be the one that is the best prepared and most resourced to endure such a drawn-out fight. The self is supplied through endless routes of suffering, overflowing anger, insatiable expectations, and lusting desires. Whereas the spirit is built up with consistent time in the word, confident prayer, serving others, and humble forgiveness. This internal fight is like watching an old boxing movie, where Ivan Drago is played by the self and the character of Rocky Balboa is the spirit – but we determine who wins by how we train and where we invest resources that will make the most impact. Do we prefer fancy equipment or an old barn out in the snow?

And he said to all, "If anyone would come after me, let him deny himself and take up his cross daily and follow me. For whoever would save his life will lose it, but whoever loses his life for my sake will save it.

Luke 9:23-24

Resources such as determination, motivation, and hard work are universally accepted to be necessary for long-term success. For things that truly matter though, sacrifice is essential. Sacrifice is a costly and risky investment – based on expectation – because it insinuates the owner has a particular attachment to the thing being given away. Because sacrificing something means that you believe in its intrinsic worth, not with words, but with actions and possessions. Expressly, there better be a reason for the sacrifice and it had better be a good one.

To sacrifice a habit or lifestyle that we value and recognize as a large part of who we are takes receptiveness, willingness, and commitment. In many ways, it is an investment in something better. This act allows and sympathizes with the belief that there is a particular value in what is being sacrificed but concedes that what we get in return is worth more than what is being given up. Invariably though, we sometimes fail to make that investment because of some lingering contention standing in our way of better. These convenient obstacles turn out to be the precise things that need to be sacrificially offered up. Just be aware, chances are they will not surrender easily, especially if you hold on to them too tightly.

BLUEPRINT FOR WAR

The battle for the self will always rage on. Some days will be manageable and routine, and other days resemble more of a bloody battlefield. Occasionally, you will make progress in one area only to find you are losing ground in another. Some days will be 1,1,1,1,1,1. Other days you will struggle to put anything other than a goose egg on the scoreboard. Understand the severity of the decision to fight against the self, as Drago said, "I must break you." The self wants to stomp out the fruits of the spirit: love, joy, peace, patience, kindness, goodness, faithfulness, gentleness, and self-control – the exact spiritual dividends we can expect in return for our sacrifices.

In attempting to perform this amputation of self, while still awake and conscious, we must understand first and foremost, things may get worse before they get better. The desires of the flesh course through our veins and arteries. After all, we have had many years of training and perfecting our warfare. But much like treating any other disease, if we address it wrongly, it comes with inherent abilities to evolve, mutate, and build resistance. More often than not, we burden the disease just enough to force it to seek a deeper root within us – the primary reason relapses occur. The inner self suffers from the *Pollyanna principle*, by hoarding the past and believing the memories to be more positive and fulfilling than they factually were.

Choosing to sacrifice the self is an activity that must become a persistent one. A continual binary decision that seamlessly blends into the next one, over the remainder of our lifetime. For example, the ticking of a clock. However obnoxious, the ticking signals a very decisive beginning and ending – both happening at the exact same moment. Memorializing the past by presently heralding the future. Consequently, as these seconds tick by, they contribute to the overall analogous waveform. The closest parallel to illustrate the principle of individual fragments contributing and blending into a total summation can be broadly observed via the passage of time, and precisely understood through the example of a shadow cast by a tree in a pasture.

As the sun petitions the horizon and slowly begins to rise, its rays fall upon the Earth. The beams radiate warmth and light, saturating the land and beckoning the dawn of a new day. Inquisitively, the rays find a lonely old oak in a field of rolling hills, ushering in the birth of a shadow. Over the course of the day, the Earth rotates while the heifers graze and slowly meander through the pasture, in no particular hurry. During the bovine hours of operation, the position, intensity, and length of that shadow from the oak tree change imperceptibly and harmoniously. This fluid transformation has all been accomplished through each tick of the clock and degree of Earth's axial rotation. Days, just like puzzles, are built one piece at a time.

What begins as one choice, can become the first step of a monumental journey. One choice leads to another, and before you know it, you have strung together a series of decisions and realize the trend of life is shifting in a new direction. Sacrifice is a choice we make every moment of every day. And thankfully for us, our Creator chose the ultimate sacrifice. In fact, Jesus sacrificed everything when He died the physical death of His creation, to save it.

And being found in human form, he humbled himself
by becoming obedient to the point of death, even
death on a cross.

Philippians 2:8

In Retrospect

Back in 1988, a 4th-grade teacher at Dana Elementary held a mock trial to determine who was guilty, for the crime of sticking gum in a boy's hair during a field trip bus ride. I just so happened to find myself as one of the plaintiffs (mostly because I indeed committed the crime). It was also in this class I remember meeting Adam. We shared an affinity for NC State Wolfpack basketball, perfecting the art of pencil fighting with Black Warriors, and drawing big rigs.

There was also a third friend, who my mother would take great pleasure in reminding him of the time he soiled himself during one of our school-famous farting contests. During these years though, most of our biggest concerns were riding Big Wheels down briar-covered banks, watching whatever Arnold Schwarzenegger movie was out, and practicing vocal impressions of the Teenage Mutant Ninja Turtles characters.

But for all three of us, we were an unknowing breed; harboring proclivities for chaos and destruction, inherited from our fathers. The days of hoping to dodge acne and voice cracking soon gave way to thoughts of a much darker nature. Somewhere, somehow, we lost our way and found ourselves descending into the darkness; separately and at times together. But, by the grace of God…

This trip down memory lane all began over 35 years ago with a group of friends. I am blessed to introduce the testimony of one of those three, the story of how God saved and redeemed my good friend Adam McCraw.

Adam McCraw

> "The roots of my testimony reach deep into the soil of my father's existence long before I was born."

In his 'prime' he was the epitome of manhood. I use quotation marks, because it is a lie sold to so many men who do not know God's heart for mankind, nor what true manhood looks like. But he was a man's man, considered the baddest in our area, and good looking to boot – which created a violent womanizer with a silver tongue – all the characteristics and dynamics, which multiplied to produce the controlling, manipulative, dominating force of pride that existed within him. To this day, even after God delivered me, I still struggle at times to not be this man. You see, I was blessed and cursed with many of the same attributes and pitfalls as my father.

While this reference to being the baddest is seen in the most positive of lights, we all come to understand that sin is fun, for a season. Then comes death – "for the wages of sin is death." His season of sin saw him revered by mostly everyone we knew. Enter the reaping, a biblical principle known by most as well, that we reap what we sow. The word of God is true and real!

He had three sons and a wife that left nothing to be desired. I was the oldest of the three, who was left with a gaping father wound when the culmination of his sowing to sin brought a harvest of devastation that rippled into not only his life but as many know, the lives of all who are in connection and many indirectly as well.

Suffice it to say, many things led up to my precipice, but the fall from the edge is what I want to focus on. And so, the sum of all his sin takes me back to where I remember hitting the side of a SWAT team sniper, begging him not to shoot my daddy, as his scope was trained on him at our old house, a residence which was now surrounded by most of the local law enforcement and specially trained units. The events that led to this moment were the usual suspects: drugs, extreme jealousy, and a scenario that was disproportionate to those choices; leading to the blind rage to kill. Through many circumstances, my father had somehow managed to take a rookie cop hostage.

Several shots rang out from a terror-filled fleeing, with one hitting its mark through my father's *manhood*. The symbolism of which has never actually dawned on me the way it just did, until writing it down and seeing those words on paper. Both sides exchanged gunfire, all while dad was still bleeding, finally resulting in his arrest after a lengthy standoff, which was brought to an end by family and friends talking him down. After he was arrested, he was transported to the hospital to take care of his *injury*. Upon leaving, he wound up with another rookie cop escorting him, go figure. The rookie made the mistake of cuffing my father's hands in front of, instead of behind him. As he opened the door to put dad in, he left himself open and unguarded just enough that dad seized the opportunity to snatch the officer's gun. Taking the officer hostage, dad then instructs him to drive to our house where a hostage standoff ensued, involving the officer, my mom, and all of the boys. Through many hours of negotiations, the kids were permitted to leave the house, which brings me back to the place where I was pleading for my dad's life. Consequently, 40 years in prison was the consolation prize for that effort.

As I alluded to earlier, these events shaped me profoundly for a long time. Like father, like son, I followed that path of destruction. But as imprinted as I was by it all – especially being 10 years old – people would speak of him with such revelry, that I unwittingly came under Satan's yoke, leading not only myself toward devastation, but others who looked up to me as well. In retrospect, my journey took me along a path eerily similar to his. It is wild to see how much our parents influence us, despite our awareness of the possibilities and vainly blubbering that we will never be "like them."

In high school, I had a love who would have been my lifelong partner and mate. I know many say this, but my soul has been tormented ever since. She would have always been true, and in that, my demise. Not having the truth of God and His principles in my life from my earthly father, a void was left so great, that I was forced to piece it together by myself. Turns out, I'm not a great puzzle guy. I repaid her loyalty to me with debauchery and unfaithfulness, always certain she would be there, and then one day she wasn't. I did all I could to arrange a meeting with her to "win her back." In my mind I knew she would never take me back; and in my mind, "win" meant *kill*. My immaturity, insecurity, lack of a moral compass, and insane jealousy grew from that evil soil and produced the fruit of rage upon our meeting and eventual rejection that deservedly came my way. If I couldn't have her, then no one would. I put her in a chokehold meant to kill and God intervened to save my life.

The car was not in park and her foot came off the brake, rolling toward a tree in the neighborhood we were in. Mentally, in some weird twist of fate, the realization of the car hitting the tree crystallized at that moment; I wouldn't get away with murder if I proceeded. I let her go and said hit the brake and she did, terrified and truly shaken.

I can't even explain where I was, my thoughts were so twisted at this point. I felt that if I made her drive around for a while, I could talk her into staying with me. God... who am I? I have asked that question so many times in my life. So, I pulled a pocket knife out to coax her into driving for a while. I loved her so much. I could never have shed her blood, it would have destroyed me – but to asphyxiate her – that was different, a strange dichotomy. However, as we were driving, her survival instinct inclined her to jump out of the car at a red light not far from a police station, a location I was oblivious that we were approaching during the drive.

When she opened the door and ran, I froze for an instant, then jumped in the driver's seat and took off, not knowing what I was going to do. I fled to my mother's house in Atlanta about three hours away. I remember thinking it was over, so why not make it over. I drove between 110 to 140 mph all the way to ATL, expecting to die in a fiery crash and if I saw blue lights before that, I resolved to still go out the same way. No crash or flashing lights ever occurred, nor was there any respite to be found at Moms. I knew I couldn't run forever, so I decided to face the music. I took the car back after the weekend, left it about 200 feet from her house, and started the walk of hopelessness, assuming it would all converge rather quickly now. When the cops picked me up about five miles from her house, they knew I was done. I knew they could sense my utter defeat and brokenness. They just put me in the car, the fighter had no fight left.

My girlfriend was still amazing, as always. She didn't press charges, but the state did. Remember, I have a name that precedes me. Even though it was years before, the deeds of my father were still fresh for them and quite the embarrassment for the police in our town. They prosecuted me, but her merciful stance was pivotal in receiving the sentence of intense probation.

After the loss of her, my life spiraled downward. Without God as my rock, and the loss of the only rock I ever had, matters compounded themselves and led me toward a path of self-destruction that so many others follow without knowing where they are headed, only looking for a "moment." What do I do at this moment? What are my next moments? Party, forget, next moment, pain. Party, forget, pain, pain. Party, forget, pain, pain, pain. Party, never forget, violence, party, violence, party, violence beyond sanity.

I was on intensive probation after the incident, but no clarity really ever came from the gravity of the situation. I made it on probation for a month or two, when I went to a party with a fairly small group of friends and some people I didn't know. One of those individuals was the owner of the property we were on and honestly, wasn't that bad of a dude. We were drinking, and I threw a bottle in the woods. He asked me not to do that, and that was all it took for me to cross the campsite and crush his face. There were girls there, and you weren't going to talk to me like that – like a sensible human being would – in front of girls.

The depravity of my pride has been the haunting echo of my life. I think it is our greatest battle in the human realm. Think about it, pride is the original sin, it is what caused Satan's fall. The greatest and most beautiful of all the angels, and it still wasn't enough. After several surgeries and a titanium plate placed in his face, he was able to testify against me in court. I praise God that he didn't die. Many more events led to my incarceration, but in efforts to keep it trimmed down enough for my friend to use in this book, we will jump to the next chapter.

In prison, many of the things seen and heard on television do happen. It can often be sensationalized, but there is much truth in the depictions. There is much violence, and my self-destructiveness only fits in all the better. I did come by some of the best friends of my life there; insane environments will cause the dross of people's character to melt away quickly, allowing for a better view. On the flip side, there are some of the worst people on this planet there, and rightfully so. I always said prison either makes you a better criminal or you assess your life and realize that you forfeit your time and money. Before release, I decided I wanted to hang on to both of these.

In the last prison camp, I found myself reunited with my father. Yeah, take that one in. What a legacy, huh? Crazy how much a son will idolize his father even when there is really nothing honorable to even grab ahold of. You have to stop and look at the word "honorable" for a second. At this point, I'm thinking we're big stuff, a badass father-son combo in prison together. It wasn't until the true Father shed light on my definitions and interpretations of manhood, that I came to realize how off-base I was. I mean, I missed it by a million miles. My pride was a raging wildfire, consuming me and the others who went along with me. The father of lies, Satan, had sold me a sh*t sandwich and convinced me it was good.

I believe God the father started His work on me in prison; not to say He hadn't been working previously for all my life. I'm not sure how it all works, but we are given free will, and then He moves in the places where free will meets truth. Our choices can lead us to a good return, or a collision with the antithesis of truth and God: evil and Satan. His spirit can use both I believe, but mostly it is a matter of how much the soil of our hearts has been prepared. A complicated equation that only God knows the solution to.

About three months before I was scheduled to be released, I was playing basketball and got into an argument with another guy (a work from God, remember pride). We were in each other's face, a no-no to anyone who has fought much. My pride had me feeling invincible, then the next thing I know I'm waking up in the prison hospital, not even sure why I'm there. Long story short, I let my pride take me for a ride. It was devastating, taking such a blow to the lie of pride I had bought into. I had never lost a fight before, what the hell just happened?

I was in a daze and went to the showers in the dorm to try to come around a little better. Crazy side note, dad was in the same dorm as me at this point, and he jumped into the shower next to me. I was torn up, but he didn't fuss at me too bad. Maybe to lighten the mood – but honestly, it was probably his pride – he showed me his *manhood* and said, "Look son, this is where your mom shot me through the willy."

It took until the following day for me to absorb how much my "status" had taken a blow. The gravity of it all was so loud in my consciousness; my dad was in the camp, my friends, and my reputation. This is where God started. You see, "God resists the proud, but gives grace to the humble." I never even knew the concept of humility until that day. Still so much had to take place for me, but that was the beginning. I was released with much back and forth in my mind regarding revenge but getting out trumped payback at that point. My release began another chapter with my friends, females, and more than likely headed toward being locked up again.

While my thinking was still askew, I was at least aware of circumstances (soil of the heart, remember). I continued chasing "something" to fill the loss of my girlfriend, my pride being knocked down, and my life in tatters. Friends and family helped me tread water, but I wasn't doing much swimming on my own. I went to a concert with a friend and got locked up that night for a violent tirade. I was a hard-rock guy, and that was part of my persona. Afterward, I was still on a path of very little truth and went to another rock concert. My friend and I always took a fifth of liquor each, but during the first show, I didn't drink as much as usual. I watched the jumbotrons and can tell you the artist and the music to this day, but the point is, on those screens were demons doing whatever they thought demons would do. I stood there, and for the first time in my life, I think the Holy Spirit was speaking to me about the reality of the battle of good and evil in the spirit realm for our souls. After this revelation, I ("This is who I am." the hard-rock guy persona) barely made it through the rest of the concert.

After that show, I took all my CDs and started to give them to the friend that went with me, but after second thought, threw them out the window of my truck, because I didn't want to send this evil to him; the shift in my thinking had begun. I was staying with a friend at this time, and on a later weekend, I went out to the club with another friend from high school. I ended up humiliating him. So badly, that I later learned he had plotted to kill me because of it. I went back to my friend's house that night, and when I woke up the next morning, I had a dream-like vision right before awakening I will never forget.

I saw myself, a crystal perfect image of me, and behind me was nothing but complete dark. Blackness all around, the kind that sucks the sound out of the frame. You see yourself, but the deafening silence is such, that you question the existence of everything – if this is indeed your destined eternity. It struck a chord in my soul so loud that I went to church with my friend and his fiancé that same morning. It made me question if God was going to sentence me to that "outer darkness"? That maybe my soul was crying out not to be sent there, to the utter darkness and utter loneliness. It still makes my eyes tear up.

Do we not all want acceptance of some kind, at the root, complete acceptance and love? What is that? Who is that? How is it possible? God. He is the only one capable of offering such a gift. A gift that is given through Jesus, the name above all names. His Son, His bridge. He says, "Come to me, all you who are weary and burdened, and I will give you rest." He began by changing all that I knew, all that I was, and all that I would ever be from then on!

Epilogue

PARTY CRASHER

Over the course of this book, we have hopefully bridged a few gaps and tightened a few screws. Despite whatever the topical concern was, the truth of the matter is that as dysfunctional of a species we have become, we are still loved by the One who created us. Whether we get a gold star for our efforts or wind up sitting outside a classroom for a parent-teacher conference, we are cherished. Although we do not always act the way we know we should, God does provide chances for us to try again. However, these opportunities are not limitlessly available. Our mortal lifespan will eventually come to an end one day, signaling the expiration of our independent decision-making.

We must work the works of him who sent me while it is day; night is coming, when no one can work.

John 9:4

Therefore, before we can – in good conscience – close out this book, we have one last concern to address: *salvation*. If you know deep in your heart that you have already embraced the gospel and are pursuing your faith, then allow the following words to inspire and guide you when God places someone who is struggling on your doorstep. If you happen to be the one who finds yourself knocking on the door, then you are indeed at the right place. Chances are you have arrived here by any one of (or a combination of) the factors we have covered: rejection, depression, exhaustion, anger, bitterness, etc. Understand that while you may have been chauffeured here in that specific vehicle, it does not terminally define who you are, unless you allow it to. God has created you to be something more than that, and if you have never been told this or have never accepted it, it is the truth of the gospel. You, however, are the only one who is capable of making the personal choice to accept this as truth. Powerfully life-changing, eternity-altering, magnificently spiritually restorative truth, that can all begin with a prayer.

Dear Father, I am a sinner. I have gone against You and rebelled, which has caused suffering, separation, and a debt I cannot pay. Please forgive me.

I believe that You love me so much, that You sent Your son, Jesus Christ to pay my debt with His death on the cross, so I would not have to be separated from You any longer. After He died, He was buried in a tomb for three days and then rose triumphantly into heaven, conquering death.

I trust in Jesus to be not only my Savior but also my Lord. And with His Holy Spirit, I can live the life You have gifted me with, in a way that would honor and reflect You. Thank you for loving me and not giving up on me.

References

Strong, James. 2009. Strong's Expanded Exhaustive Concordance of the Bible. Nashville: Thomas Nelson.

Staton, Joshua. 2020. Overcome - Biblical Responses to Destructive Reactions: Leaders Edition. Hendersonville: Cabin in the Woods Publishers.

Page 10: Book Series Title
Packard, Edward. 1979. Choose Your Own Adventure: The Cave of Time. New York: Bantam Books.

Page 37: Statistics
Adaa.org. 2015. Facts & Statistics | Anxiety and Depression Association of America, ADAA.

Page 41: Provatio Boni
Epictetus, and Thomas Wentworth Higginson. 1955. The Enchiridion. Indianapolis: Bobbs-Merrill Educational Pub.

Page 50: 10,000 hours
Gladwell, Malcolm. 2008. Outliers: The Story of Success. New York: Little, Brown and Co.

Page 52: Oregon Trail
Bouchard, R. Philip. 1984. The Oregon Trail. Minnesota: MECC.

Page 83: "But wait, there's more!"
Valenti, Ed. 1975. Ginsu knives infomercial. Rhode Island: Dial Media, Inc.

Page 105-106: Philanthropy
Chernow, Ron. 1999. Titan: the life of John D. Rockefeller, Sr. New York: Vintage Books.

Page 130: Talking to a volleyball
Zemeckis, Robert, William Broyles, Steve Starkey, Tom Hanks, Jack Rapke, Joan Bradshaw, Don Burgess, et al. 2002. Cast away. Beverly Hills, CA: 20th Century Fox Home Entertainment.

Page 133: Felis Catus
Barker, Bob. 1979. The Price is Right. CBS/Viacom

Page 150: A beaut'
Stanton, John, Steve Irwin, and Terri Irwin. 2001. Crocodile Hunter's Croc Files.

Page 174: Quote on pride
Lewis, C. S. 1960. Mere Christianity. New York: Macmillan.

Page 186: Obnoxious show tunes
Adams, Lee, Charles Strouse. 1960. Bye Bye Birdie

Page 189: Chunk
Spielberg, Steven, Chris Columbus, Harvey Bernhard, Richard Donner, Sean Astin, Josh Brolin, Jeff B. Cohen, et al. 2010. The Goonies. Burbank, Calif: Warner Bros. Entertainment, Inc.

Page 201, 203: "I must break you."
Stallone, Sylvester. 1985. Rocky IV. United States: MGM/UA Entertainment Company.

Strategic Discipleship

Strategic Discipleship is a unique approach to address and confront substance abuse and addiction. Far too often programs and support groups place too much importance on recovery instead of a relationship with the Savior. While we believe this trend occurs unintentionally, we must stop and ask ourselves, "Which is the more important issue, sobriety or salvation?"

Our responsibility is to share the Gospel of Jesus Christ in whatever ministry field we find ourselves called to. And, as Matthew 28 points out, we are also called to make disciples. What a beautifully advantageous intersection of purpose and possibility God has provided us with to fulfill that calling in the specific ministry of substance abuse.

This opportunity began by observing the deficiency of available resources for individuals and organizations motivated to address the issue of addiction and substance abuse wreaking spiritual havoc on communities nationwide. As a result, in April of 2021, Cabin in the Woods Publishers began to align their company model to focus more on equipping communities to combat substance abuse in a biblically meaningful way.

Our method for equipping ministries, non-profit organizations, churches, and small group leaders with guidance and materials for starting and maintaining Christian faith-based recovery support is outlined through what we call Strategic Discipleship. Made up of four components, our system is designed for each stage to successively build upon the previous ones, with the intent of shifting the identity of the recovering individual from active addiction to godly purpose.

Overcome – Biblical Responses to Destructive Reactions
Introductory level designed to meet individuals where they are, spiritually and emotionally, by addressing many of the reactions that are responsible for addiction and chaos in our lives. Destructive reactions are contrasted against a proper biblical response, in hopes of moving the individual through recovery and their spiritual walk.

The Resistance – Becoming a Servant Leader through the Beatitudes
In the second installment, the recovering individual is then guided through an in-depth study on the Beatitudes, to encourage them to begin addressing residual and reoccurring issues in their lives, by confronting the self and developing their character.

Align – A Modern Dissection of the Human Heart
Since it is the motivator, the third stage seeks to educate the individual on the spiritual and metaphysical driving force of the heart. In doing so, we spiritually encourage those in recovery to become aware of and harness the impactful power of the organ that beats in their chest.

Blueprint – The Builder's Mindset
Throughout each level, the recovering individual has been progressively building their new identity in Christ. And in the final study, they are guided toward finding their substantial purpose – as God designed them – and has equipped them as such.

Available from Cabin in the Woods

Overcome - Leaders Edition
Paperback
8x10
Published September 2020
ISBN 979-8657481594
Available on Amazon

This Leaders Edition is packed
with every thing an individual,
ministry or organization needs to
begin support groups to minister
to individuals in recovery from
substance abuse.

The Resistance - Second Edition
Paperback
5x8
Published December 2020
ISBN 979-8682867264
Available on Amazon

The Resistance is a Christian
leadership course based on the
beatitudes as Jesus taught during
the sermon on the mount. In this
book, we strive to become better
servant leaders by tackling the
disease of self.

Thank you for your purchase!
We are an independent Christian publisher and your support
allows us to continue our mission. All profits are invested back
into the growth of the company. If you would like to continue
to support us, please subscribe to our mailing list to get updates
on new projects, releases and special offers.

Visit: www.cabininthewoodspublishers.com/subscribe
Follow: @cabininthewoodspublishers

JOHN 6 37

PHILIPPIANS 1 6

JOHN 14 18

JEREMIAH 17 9

1 PETER 2 11

MATTHEW 6 33

JOSHUA 1 9

OVER
CO
ME

JEREMIAH 29 11

GALATIANS 5 1

PROVERBS 11 2

MATTHEW 11 28

EPHESIANS 2 10

1 PETER 5 8

PSALM 147 3

MATTHEW 6 27

JOHN 16 33

ROMANS 12 2